BRICK
BEASTS

BRICK
BEASTS

40 CLEVER AND CREATIVE IDEAS TO MAKE FROM CLASSIC LEGO®

KEVIN HALL

BARRON'S

A Quintet Book

First edition for the United States and Canada published in 2017 by Barron's Educational Series, Inc.

All inquiries should be addressed to:
Barron's Educational Series, Inc.
250 Wireless Boulevard
Hauppauge, NY 11788
www.barronseduc.com

Library of Congress Control Number: 2016962961
ISBN 978-1-4380-1091-5
QTT.BKITM

This book was conceived, designed, and produced by
Quintet Publishing Limited
Ovest House
58 West Street
Brighton, East Sussex
BN3 1DD
United Kingdom

Photographer: Neal Grundy
Designers: Anna Gatt, Michelle Rowlandson
Project Editors: Kath Stathers, Leah Feltham
Editorial Director: Emma Bastow
Publisher: Mark Searle

9 8 7 6 5 4 3 2 1

Printed in China by C & C Offset Printing Co Ltd.

welcome to BRICK BEASTS

A lot of the time when I am at an event displaying my LEGO® brick models, I am asked if my models and sculptures are created using special parts, or if I get unique parts made especially for a particular model. The answer is that the parts I use are the exact same parts that you get in the LEGO sets you purchase in the stores. This book is to show just that.

The models in this book are all based on mythological and fantastical beasts. I have used my imagination to create them using fun and interesting colors and shapes.

On the whole, they have been created using the basic parts that you will find in the CLASSIC boxes, which of course aren't just classic 2 x 4 bricks, but include slopes, plates, tiles, and even tiny 1 x 1 round tiles with eyes printed on them. However, because mythical beasts can be quite intricate, some of the finer details have been created using parts from other LEGO sets such as Mixels and Creator. Many of the teeth and curved slopes that I've used, for example, come from Mixel sets, while horns are found in many Creator kits.

When I am building my models, I always love the challenge of creating a model using the parts I have at hand. So, don't worry if you haven't got the exact pieces I list. Just like any LEGO builder, you can be creative and re-create the models in this book to suit the parts you have in your own collection. Remember, there is no right or wrong way of building with LEGO, as long as you have fun creating the models. That is the most important thing.

—Kevin Hall, Brick Galleria Ltd

contents

sphinx

While the Egyptian sphinx has the body of a lion and the head of a man, the one in Greek mythology is altogether more elaborate with the body of a lion, the head of a woman, a serpent-headed tail, and wings. I've used a headlight brick attached to a jumper plate to make the nose look like the sphinxes of Greek sculpture.

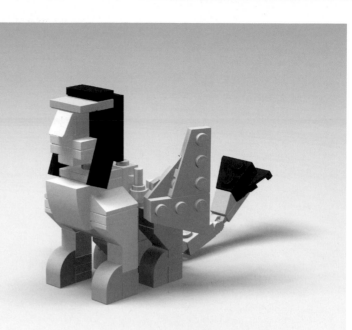

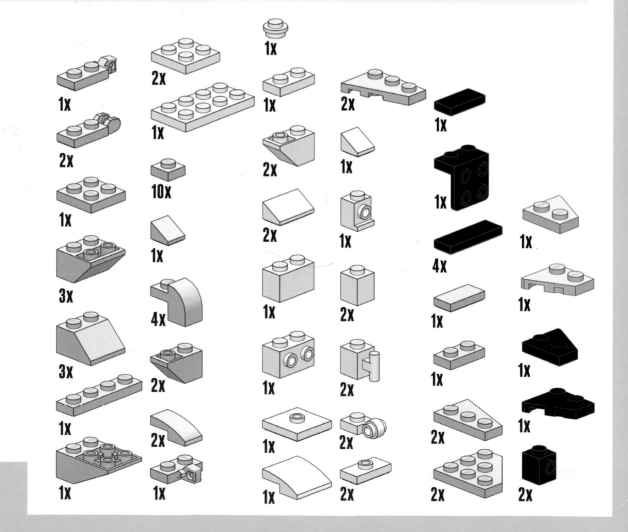

SPHINX

1

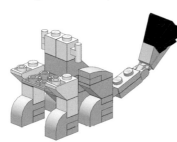

2

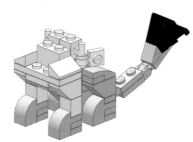

3

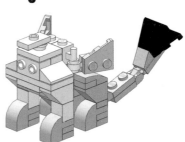

4

5

6

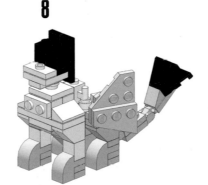

7

8

9

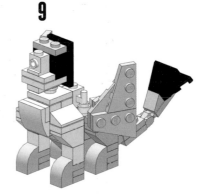

10

minotaur

The Minotaur has the torso of a very muscular man and the head, tail, and legs of a bull. He lived on the island of Crete, imprisoned in a labyrinth—a maze of a house. He was killed by Theseus, who used a ball of thread to guide himself back out of the labyrinth after he had slain the beast. Give the Minotaur well-defined stomach muscles using 1 x 2 tiles spaced apart.

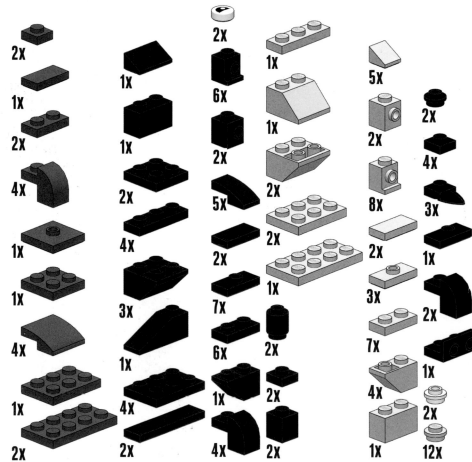

MINOTAUR

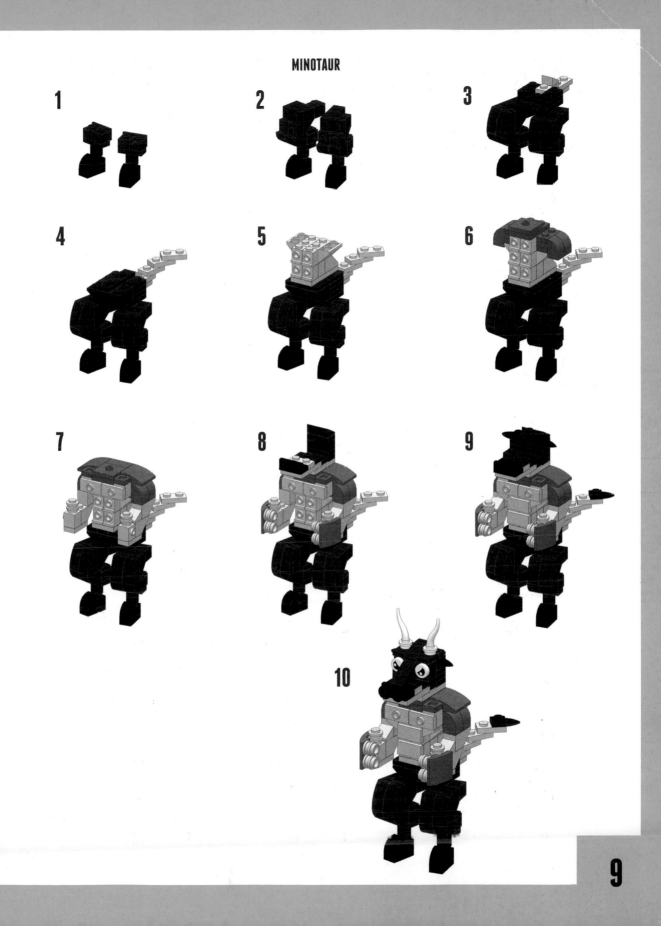

zombie

Zombies originally come from Haiti, where they are dead bodies brought back to life through the use of magic. They then become the slave of the person who brought them to life. I've used two different styles of eyes to give it a typically zombie-like expression. Curved 1 x 2 bricks make the model look as if it is reaching out to you with drooping zombie hands.

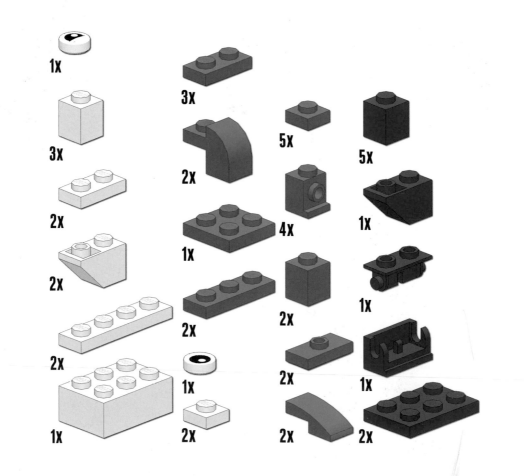

1x

3x

2x

2x

2x

1x

3x

2x

1x

2x

1x

2x

5x

4x

2x

2x

2x

5x

1x

1x

1x

2x

ZOMBIE

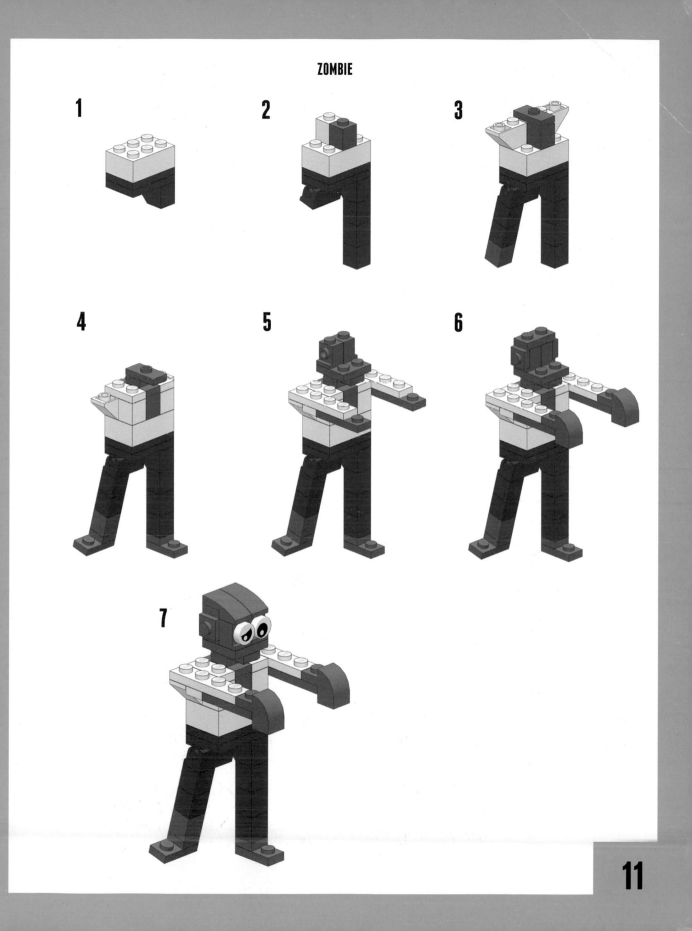

jackalope

A jack rabbit with an antelope's horns, the jackalope comes from North American folklore but actually resembles a hare more than a rabbit. It is said to be able to imitate the human voice. Hunters often lure the jackalope from its lair with whiskey. The antlers are made using inverse slopes, and the whiskers by using 1 x 1 plates with horizontal clips turned on their sides.

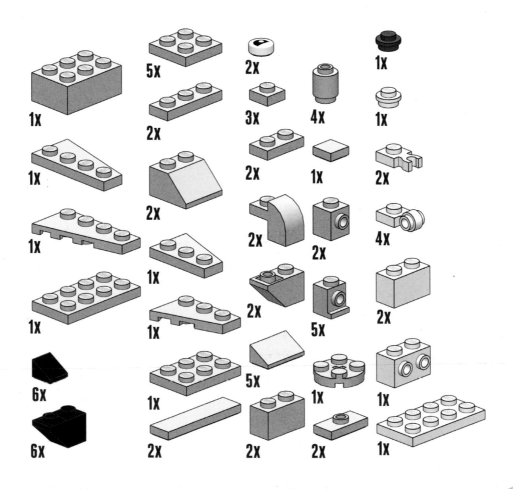

JACKALOPE

1

2

3

4

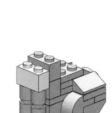

5

6

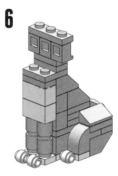

7

8

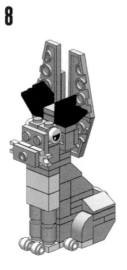

9

ninki nanka

The Ninki Nanka lives in the swamps of West Africa. In Gambia its name roughly translates as "dragon devil," and it is described as having the body of a crocodile, the neck of a giraffe, and the head of a horse. It comes out of the swamp at night and eats anything in its path. Alternating the small 1 x 1 slopes on its back gives it authentic-looking crocodile skin.

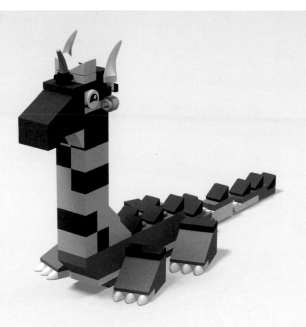

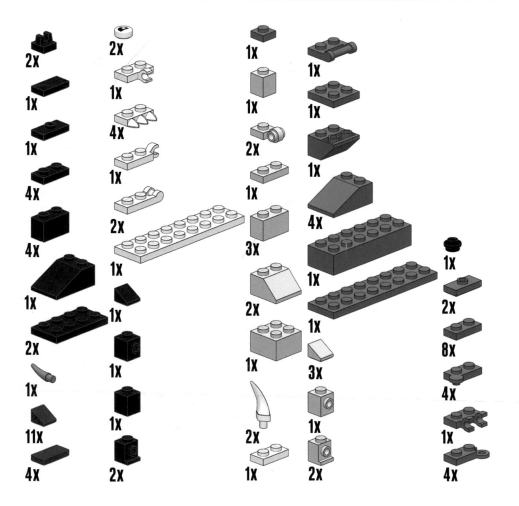

2x 2x 1x 1x

1x 1x 1x 1x

1x 4x 1x 1x

4x 1x 2x 1x

4x 2x 1x 4x

1x 1x 1x 1x

2x 1x 2x 1x 2x

1x 1x 2x 8x

11x 1x 2x 1x 4x

4x 2x 1x 2x 1x

4x

NINKI NANKA

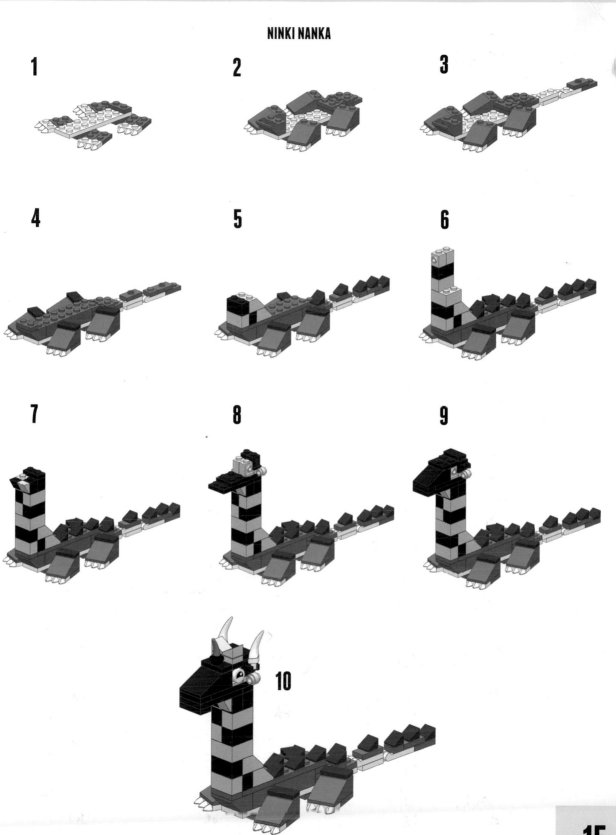

ahuizotl

The ahuizotl comes from Aztec mythology. It is a dog-like creature with five hands—one of which is on the end of its tail, which it uses to grab its prey. It is said to be fond of eating humans, especially their nails, eyes, and teeth. I've used 1 × 2 plates connected together to make its tail flexible.

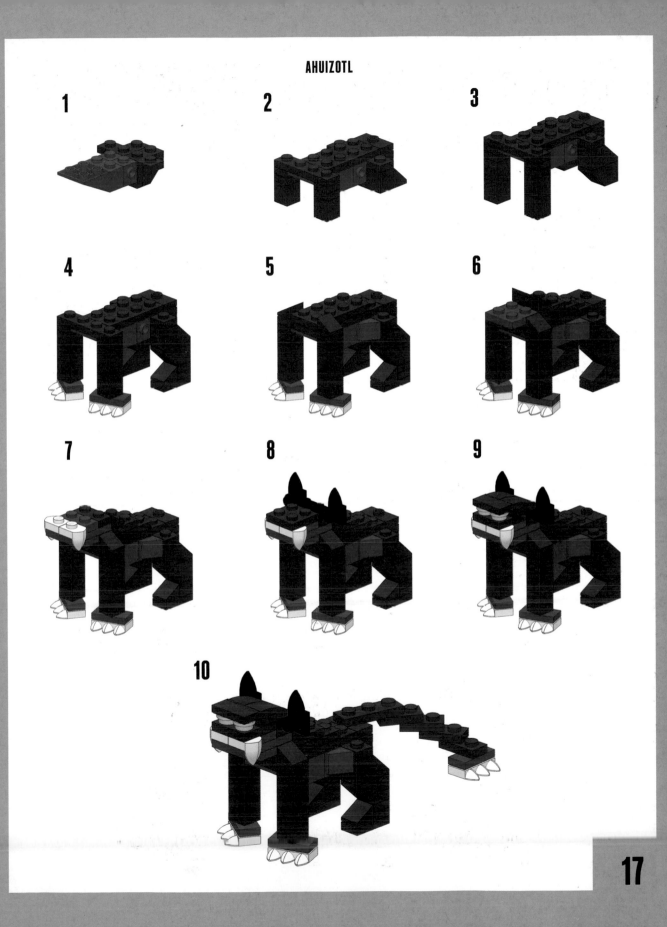

imp

Less evil than a goblin, imps are generally mischievous rather than outright bad. Their origins lie in German folklore, where they often play jokes on humans as a way to get their attention and in the hope of making friends with them. You can mount the imp on a stack of clear bricks to make it look like it's flying, as I have done here.

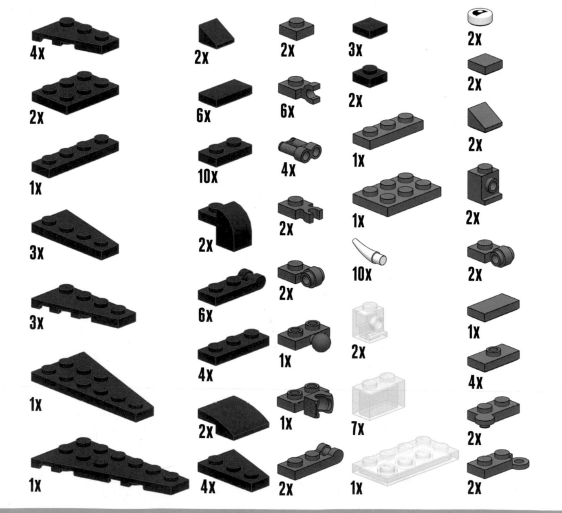

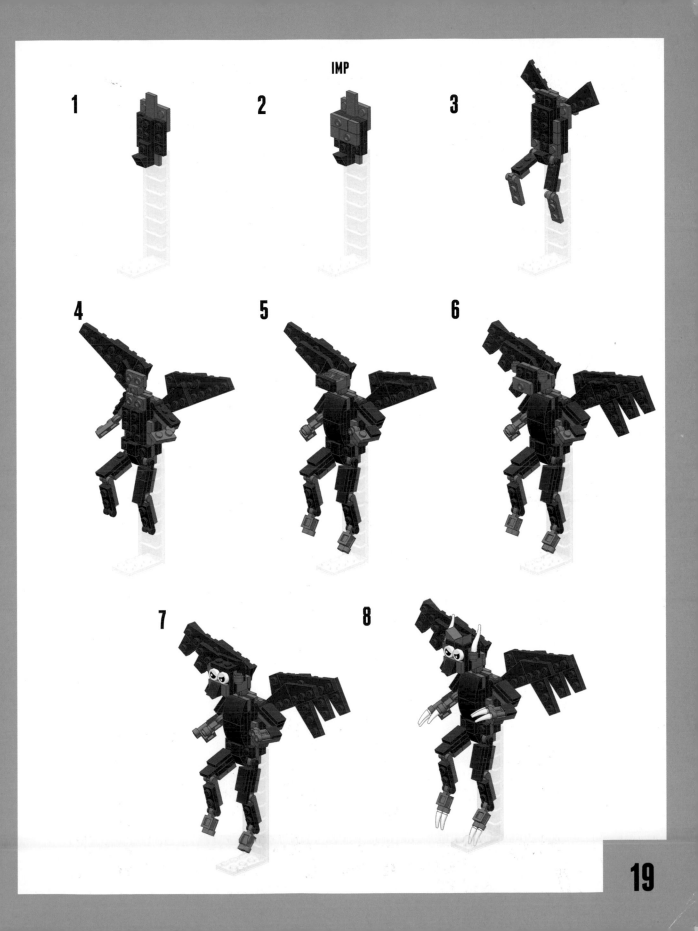

IMP

19

gorgon

With hair made of living snakes and with a hideously ugly face, gorgons turn anyone who looks at them into stone. A popular figure in Greek mythology, the most famous gorgon is Medusa. She was killed by Perseus, who used a mirror to look at her reflection instead of at the real thing so as to avoid being turned to stone. Her hair is made of LEGO® snakes, which come in the collectible mini-figures and Batman™ sets. I've attached them using 1 x 1 modified tiles with clips.

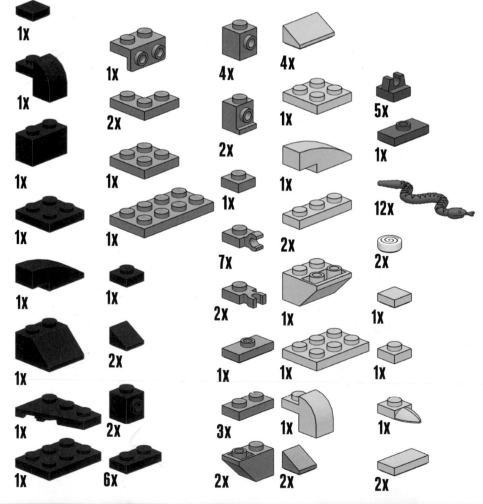

1x
1x
1x
1x
1x
1x
1x
1x
2x
1x

1x
2x
1x
1x
7x
2x

4x
2x
1x
1x
1x
2x
1x

4x
1x
1x
2x
1x
1x
3x
1x
2x
2x

5x
1x
12x
2x
1x
1x
1x
2x

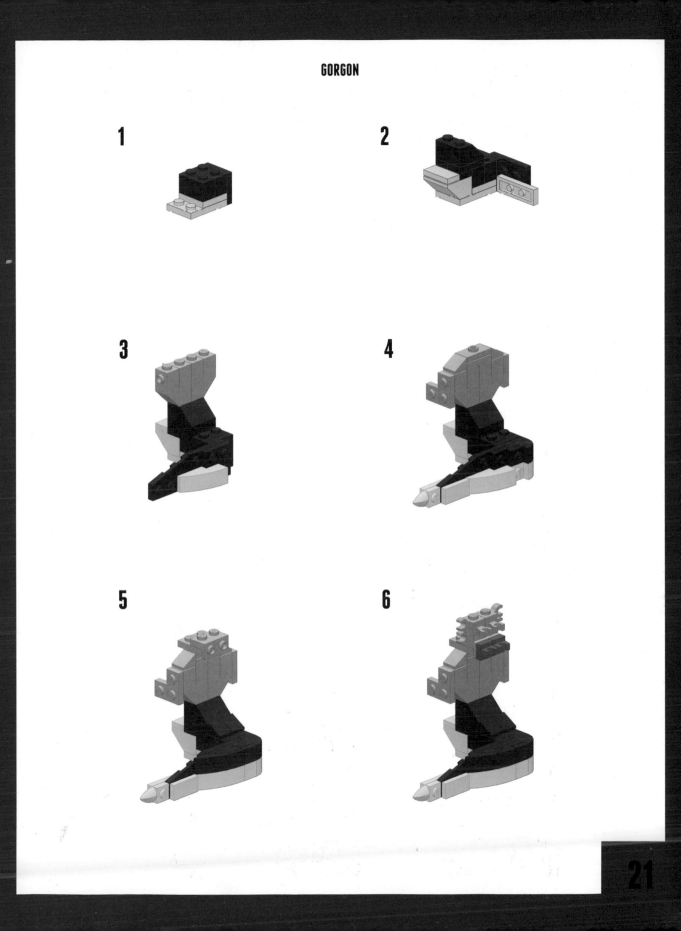

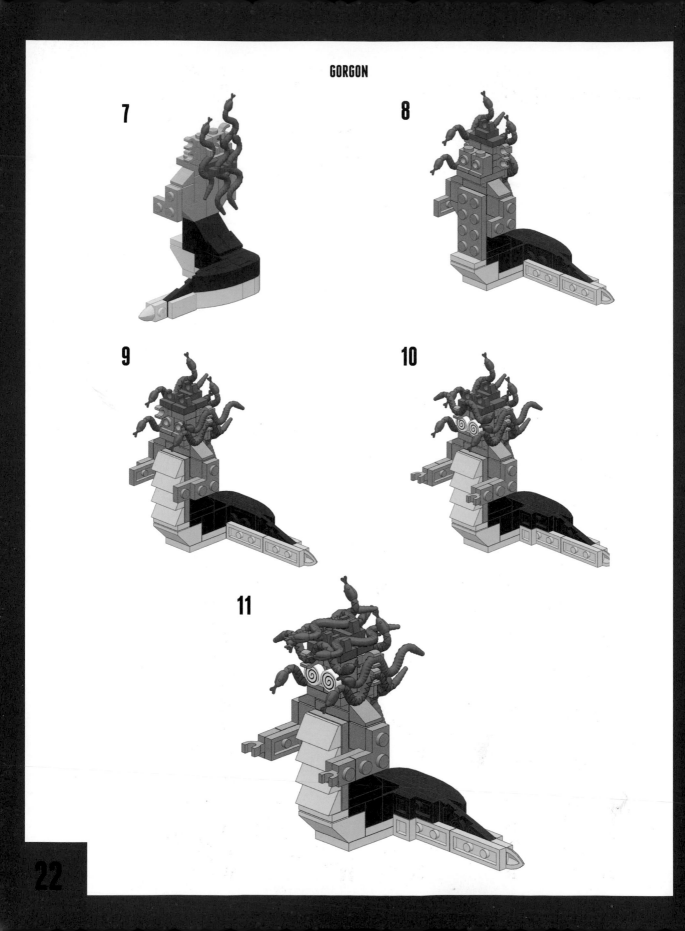

cockatrice

The cockatrice is a deadly beast from European mythology that can kill people, animals, and plants just by looking at them. It has the head of a cockerel and the body of a dragon or a two-legged serpent. It can only be killed by a weasel or by hearing a cock crow. To make the head taper into the body, I've added tiles to the neck.

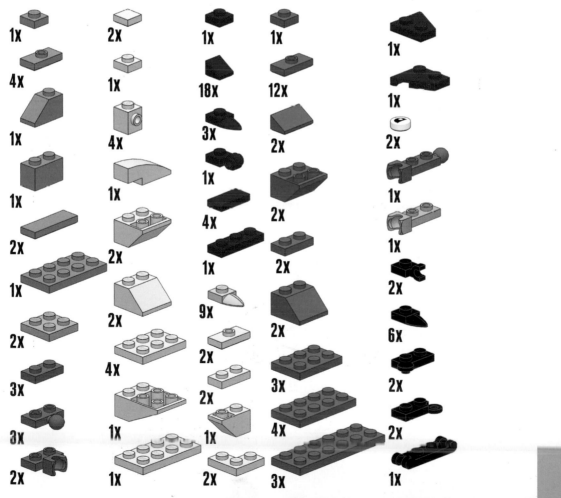

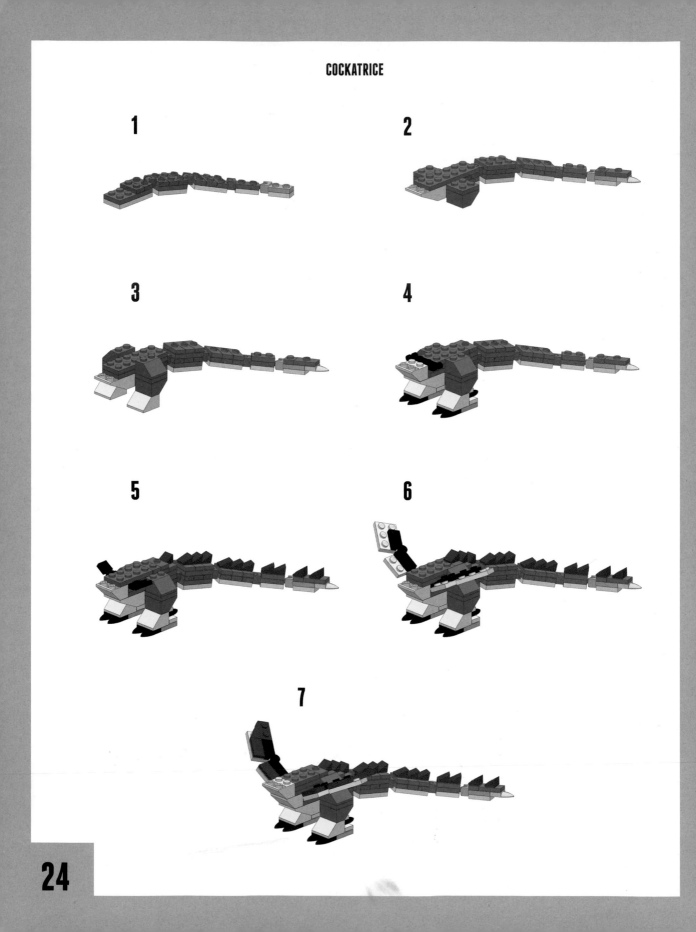

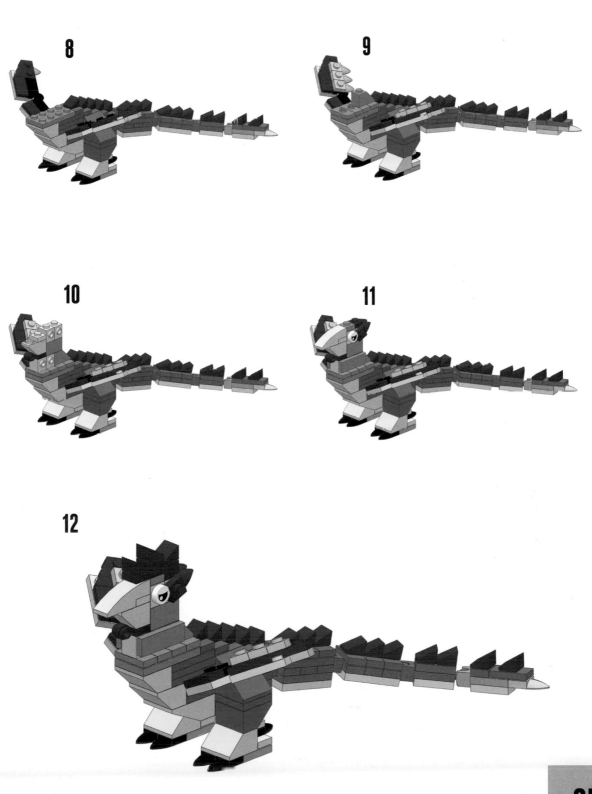

kraken

This giant monster of the seas is found off the coast of Norway. It resembles a giant octopus, and although it usually lurks in the depths, when it does rise to the surface it can cause huge waves to ripple outward and is capable of attacking whole ships. I've used a 2 × 2 modified plate with an octagonal bar frame to attach the eight legs and give them free movement.

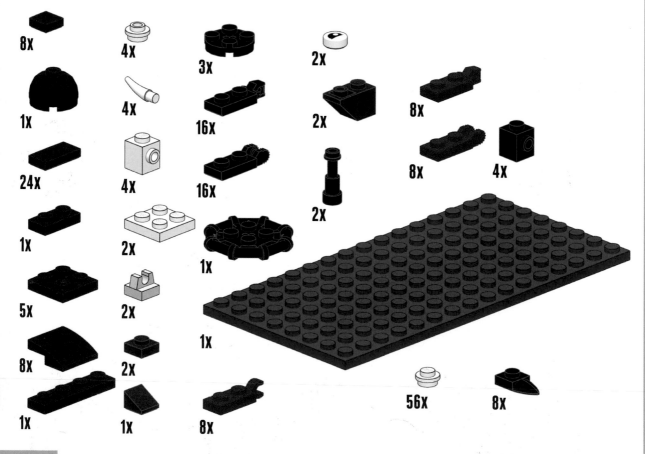

8x

4x

3x

2x

1x

4x

16x

2x

8x

24x

4x

16x

8x

4x

1x

2x

1x

2x

5x

2x

1x

8x

2x

56x

8x

1x

1x

8x

KRAKEN

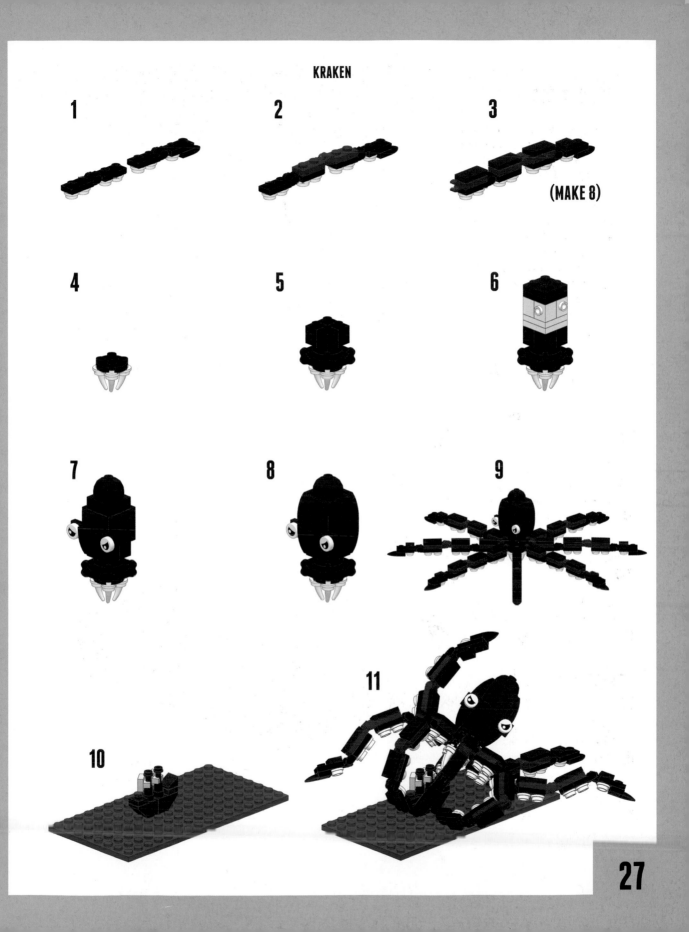

1

2

3

(MAKE 8)

4

5

6

7

8

9

11

10

27

unicorn

With its spiraling horn and sleek body, the unicorn is an elegant creature that can only be tamed by a young and innocent woman. It has magical powers that can heal illnesses. Hunters are keen to capture these beasts so that they can sell the horn for money. I've used inverse slopes and regular slopes on the legs to make it look as if it's trotting.

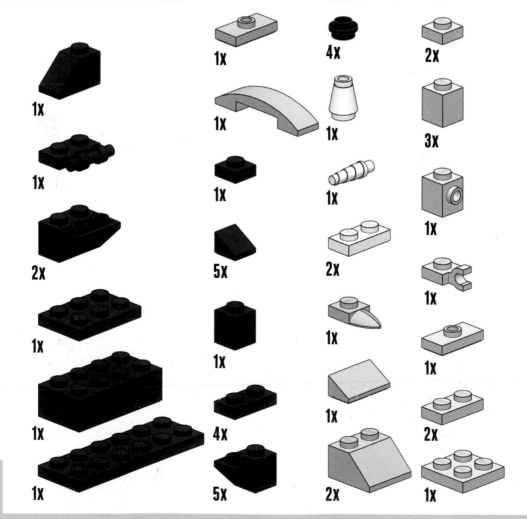

1x 1x 4x 2x

1x 1x 1x 3x

1x 1x 1x 1x

2x 5x 2x 1x

1x 1x 1x 1x

1x 4x 1x 2x

1x 5x 2x 1x

UNICORN

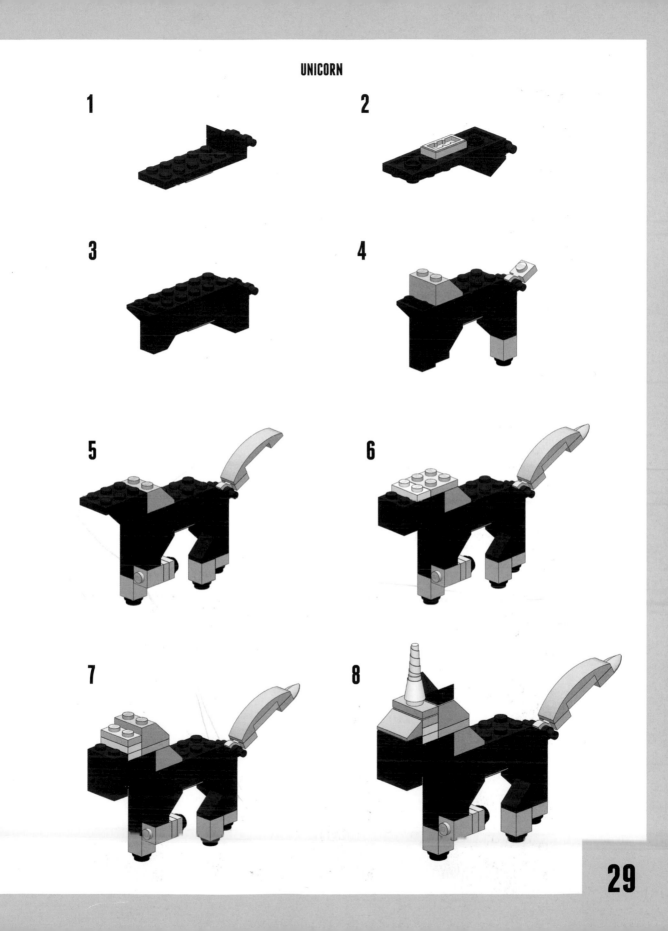

29

satyr

Its lower half is that of a goat, yet it has the torso, arms, and head of a human. Commonly found in the hillside forests of Greek mythology, satyrs are fond of drinking wine and chasing women and are usually found playing a flute or a pan-pipe. The legs are built upside down to create uniquely satyr-shaped legs.

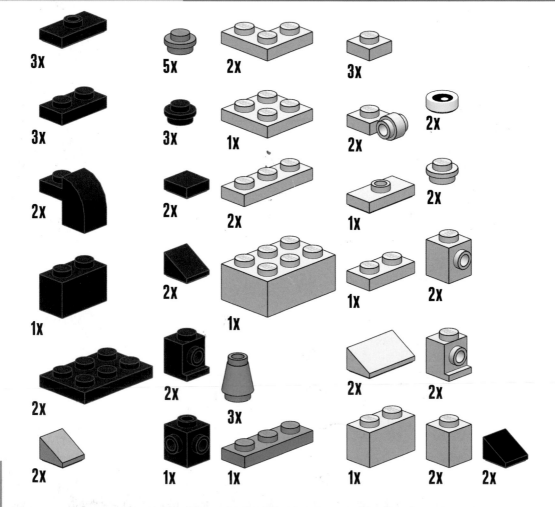

3x

3x

2x

1x

5x

3x

2x

2x

2x

2x

1x

2x

2x

1x

2x

3x

2x

2x

1x

1x

1x

3x

3x

2x

2x

1x

2x

1x

2x

2x

2x

1x

2x

2x

SATYR

sea-goat

The sea-goat, with the head and forelegs of a goat and the body and tail of a fish, is forever immortalized in the Capricorn zodiac sign. The fins at the back are attached to the tail using I x I plates with horizontal clips facing in each direction. The smooth, curved horns on the side of the head are made using claws.

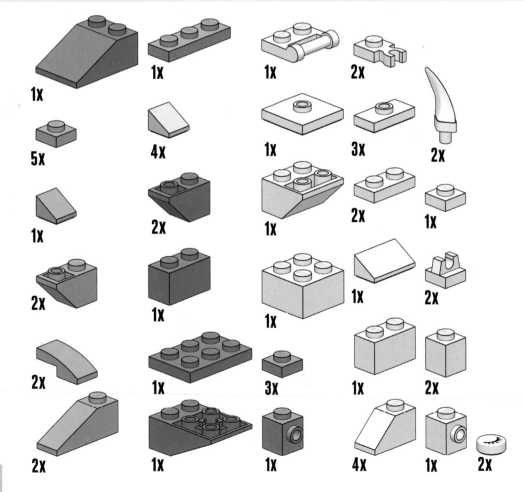

1x

1x

1x

2x

5x

4x

1x

3x

2x

1x

2x

1x

2x

1x

2x

1x

1x

1x

2x

2x

1x

3x

1x

2x

2x

1x

1x

4x

1x

2x

SEA-GOAT

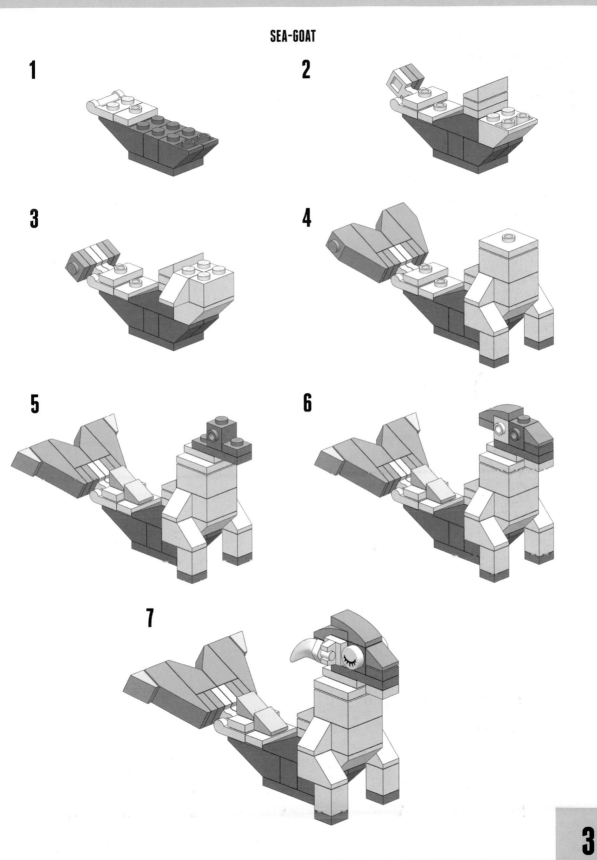

goblin

There is rarely anything friendly about a goblin. These mischievous fellows from European folklore are usually small, ugly, and greedy for other people's gold and jewelry. They often have magical powers, although they don't use them for good. Make his big pointy feet with a 1 × 3 plate with a 1 × 1 slope on the end.

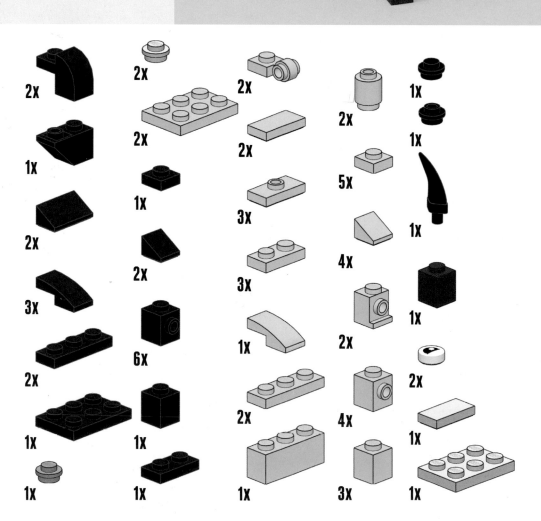

GOBLIN

phoenix

This red and gold bird resembles a large eagle, but it has one amazing ability—it never truly dies. Instead, it combusts into ashes from which a new phoenix will rise. The phoenix represents the cycle of life and is often linked with the sun. The transparent orange slopes used on the tips of the feathers add to this appearance.

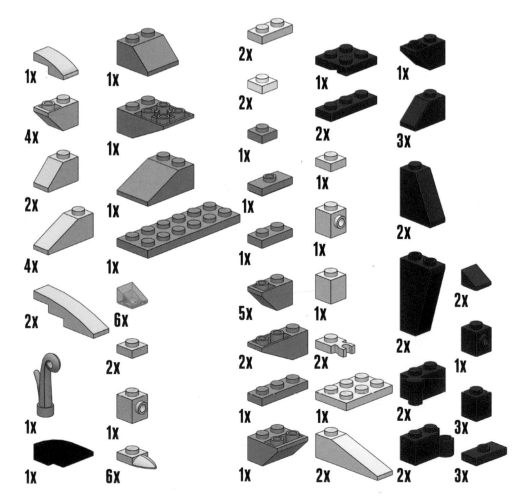

PHOENIX

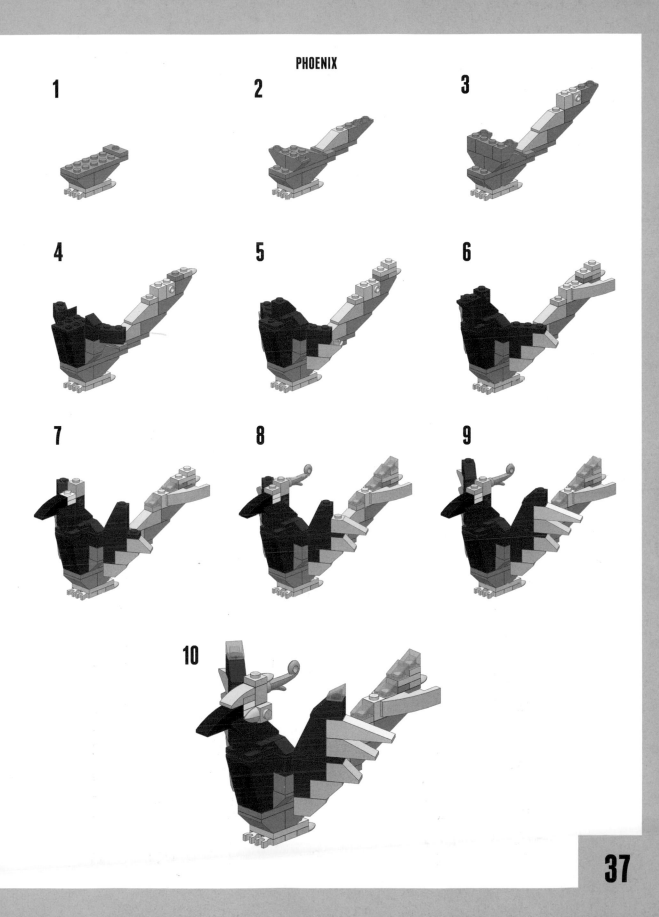

cyclops

Their name translates as "round eye," but cyclops were in fact giants in Greek and Roman mythology with one large eye in the middle of their foreheads. In Homer's "Odyssey"—an epic Greek poem—the hero Odysseus blinds a cyclops by driving a stake through his eye. If you use a hinge plate, you can space the big toe slightly farther away from the others to create more realistic giant feet.

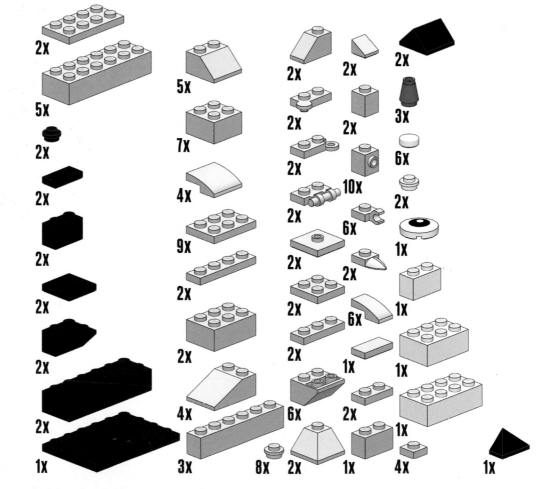

CYCLOPS

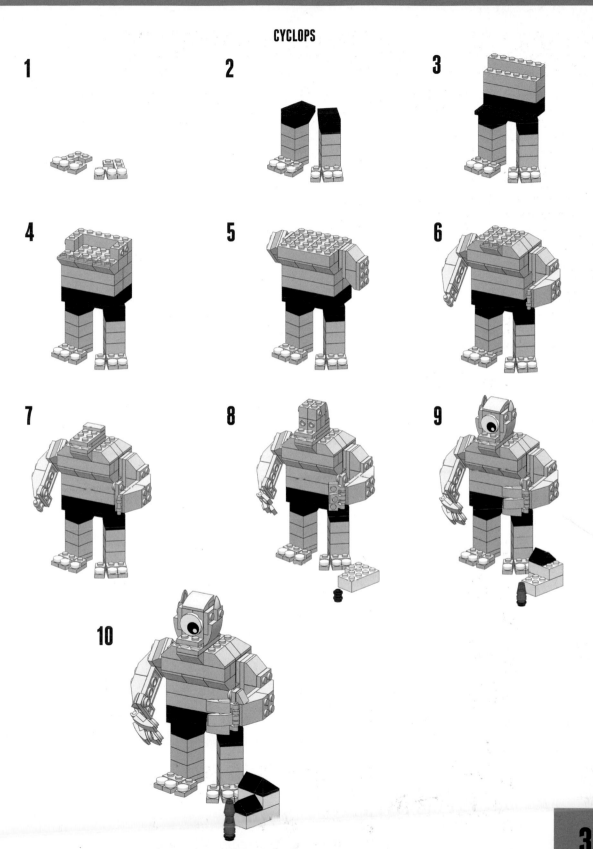

troll

Trolls come from Norse mythology and tend to live far away from humans in caves or mountains. They are sometimes giant and sometimes small, but generally are not very bright. They live underground, and if they come into contact with sunlight they turn to stone. Use flat 1 x 1 round tiles to make troll-like toes.

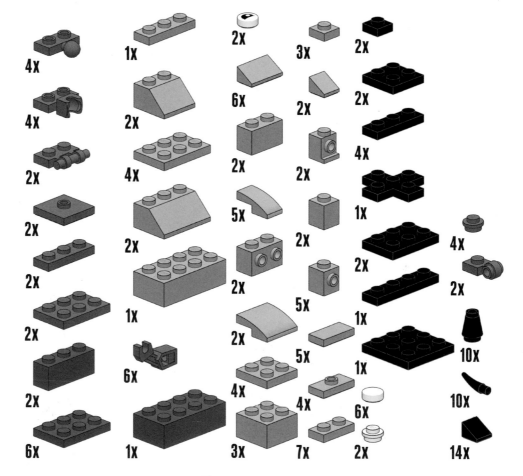

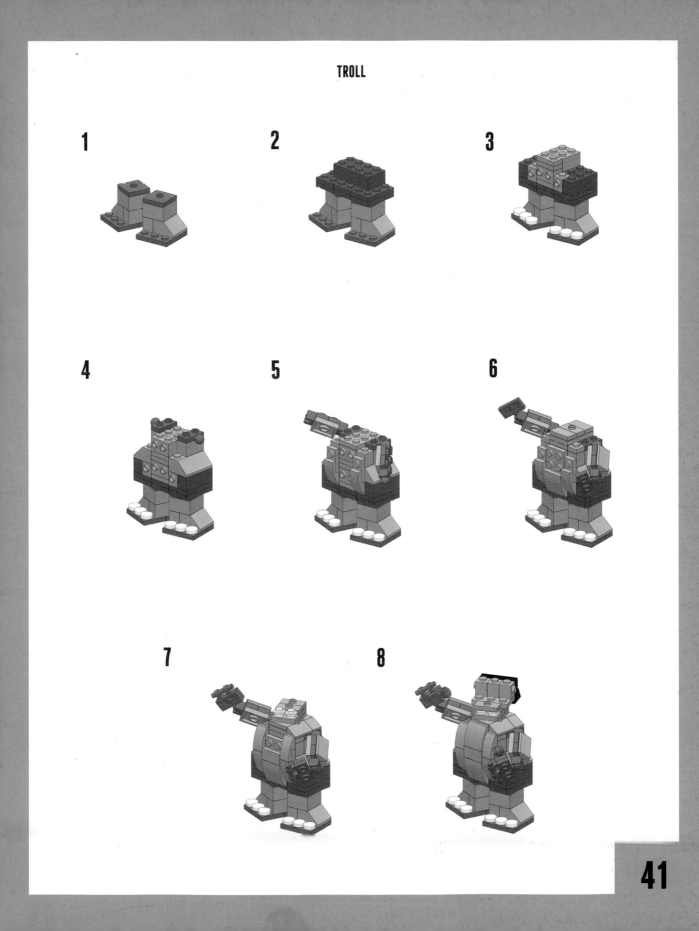

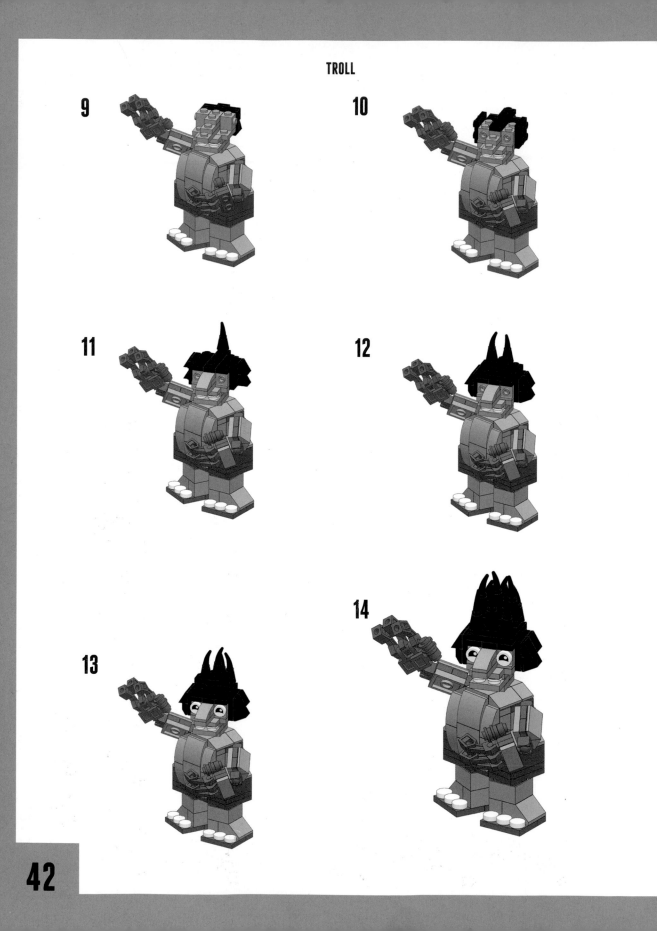

dragon

Dragons come in many different forms, as they have featured in mythology all over the world. In Europe, they are usually winged and could often breathe fire, while in Asia they were generally long-bodied but wingless. This one is European and has wings, which are created using a ball and socket joint at the body and a click hinge in the middle so they can fold and flap.

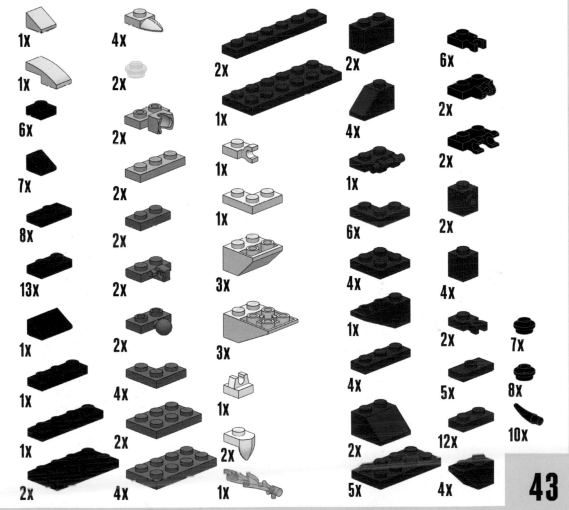

1x
1x
6x
7x
8x
13x
1x
1x
1x
2x

4x
2x
2x
2x
2x
2x
2x
4x
2x

2x
1x
1x
1x
1x
3x
3x
1x
2x
1x

2x
4x
1x
4x
1x
6x
4x
1x
4x
2x
5x

6x
2x
2x
2x
4x
2x
5x
12x
4x

7x
8x
10x

DRAGON

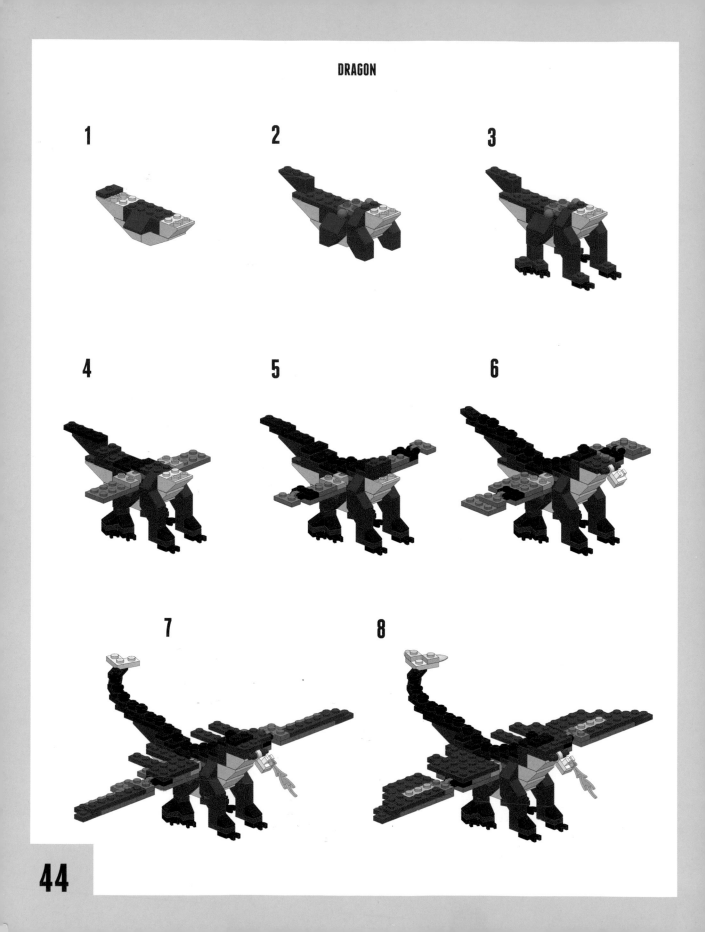

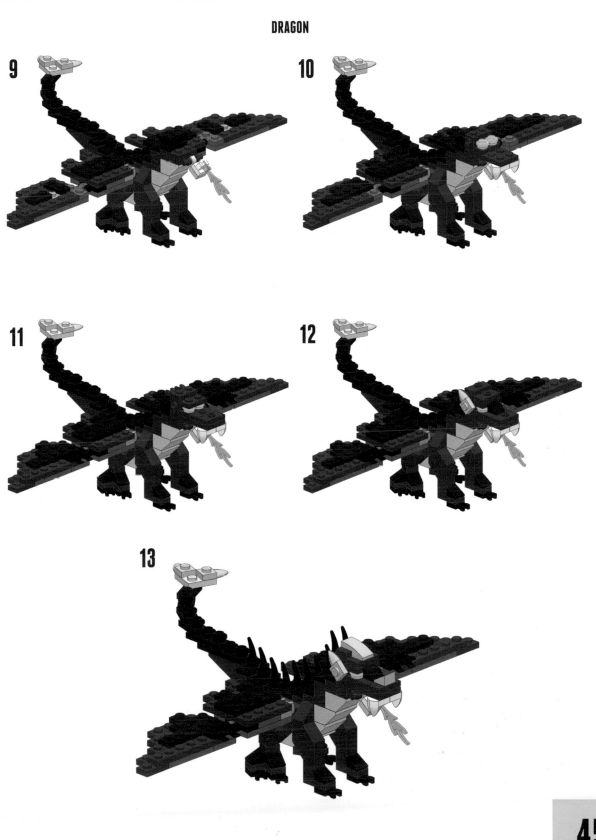

yowie

The yowie is a shy and secretive creature that dwells in the Australian wilderness. It walks upright on two very large feet and can be anywhere from the height of a man to twice as tall. It is sometimes said to have flowing white hair that covers its features. Use 2 x 3 wedge plates to give the creature its mammoth feet.

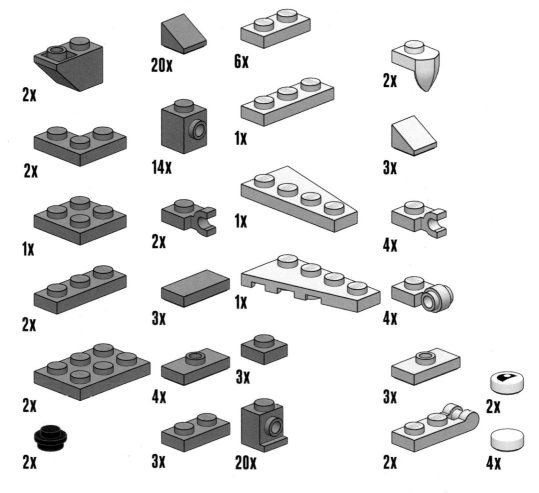

2x

20x

6x

2x

2x

14x

1x

3x

1x

2x

1x

4x

2x

3x

1x

4x

2x

4x

3x

3x

2x

2x

3x

20x

2x

4x

YOWIE

vampire

Originating in the folklore of eastern Europe, vampires are human-like in form but are really "undead," feeding off the blood of the living. Those they bite are then turned into vampires themselves. Make the cape separately from the body and attach it using a 1 × 1 brick with a stud on its side.

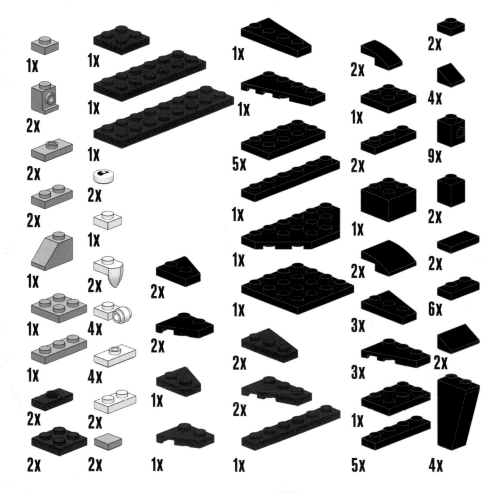

1X

1X

2X

2X

2X

1X

1X

1X

2X

2X

1X

2X

1X

2X

1X

2X

4X

1X

4X

2X

2X

2X

1X

2X

1X

2X

1X

2X

1X

5X

1X

1X

1X

2X

1X

2X

1X

2X

1X

1X

2X

2X

1X

2X

1X

3X

3X

1X

5X

2X

4X

9X

2X

2X

2X

6X

2X

4X

VAMPIRE

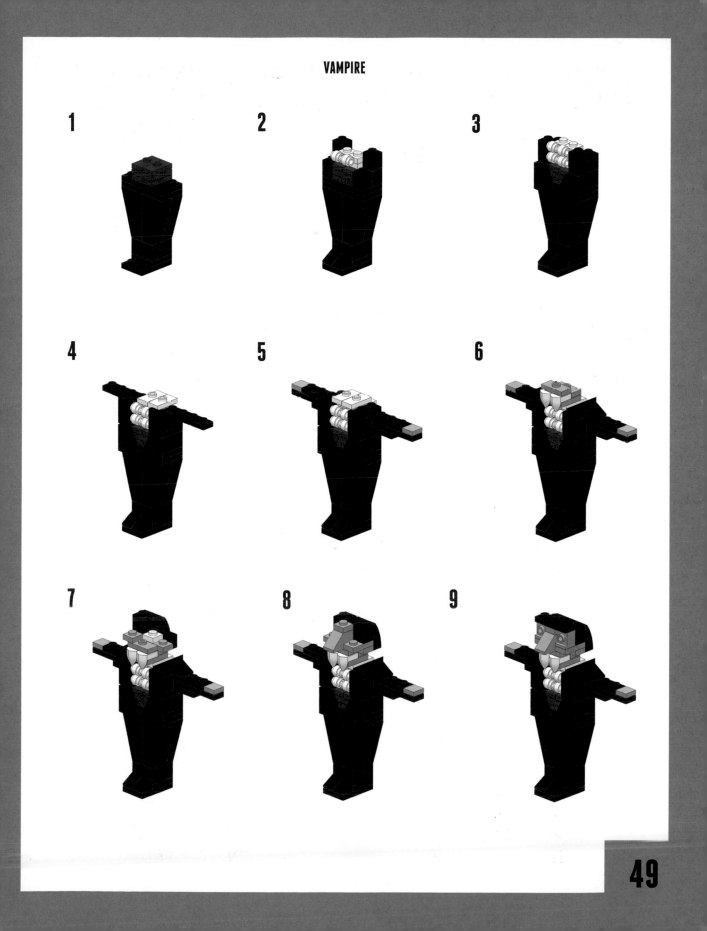

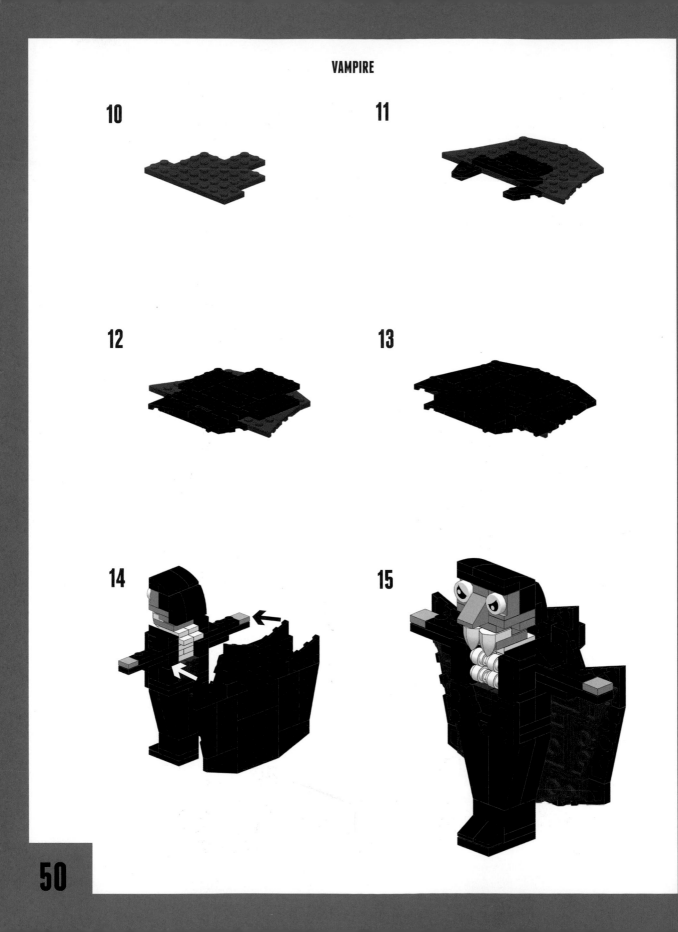

kitsune

With its origins in Japanese folklore, the kitsune is a very smart fox that can shape-shift into human form. The older and wiser a kitsune is, the more tails it has, with the most being nine. When it grows its ninth tail, its fur often becomes white. Create the narrow foxy snout by using a jumper so it can be one stud wide.

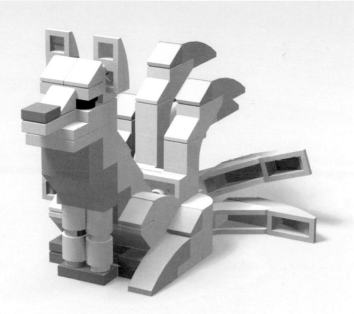

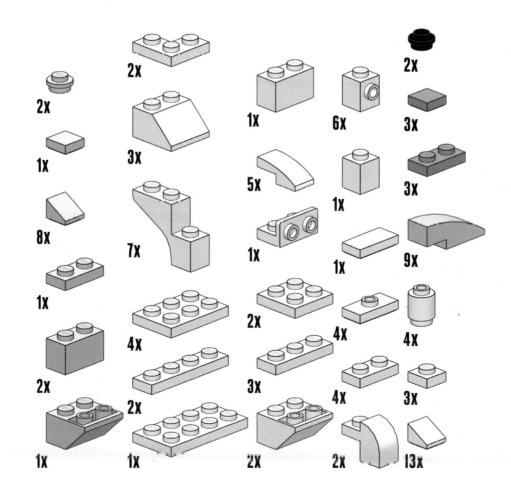

2x
1x
8x
1x
2x
1x

2x
3x
7x
4x
2x
1x

2x
5x
1x
1x

1x
6x
1x

2x
3x
2x

2x
4x
3x
4x

2x
2x

2x
3x
3x
9x
4x
3x
13x

KITSUNE

1

2

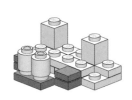

3

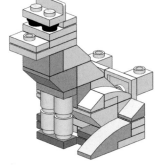

4

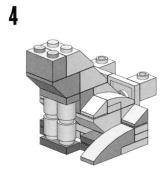

5

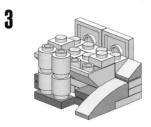

6

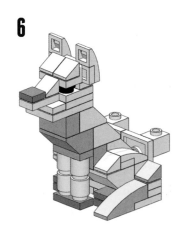

7

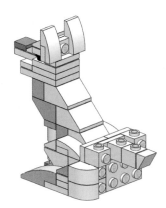

KITSUNE

8

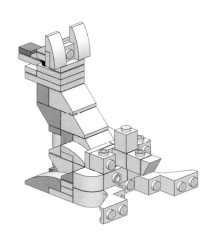

9

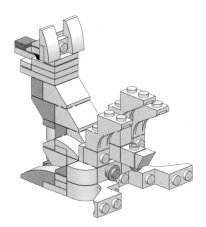

10

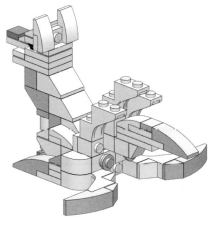

11

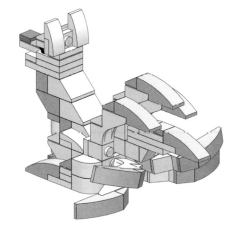

12

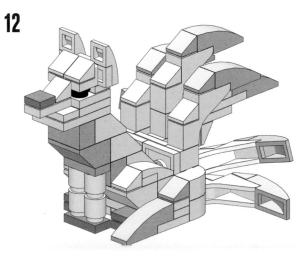

basilisk

This crested snake has its roots in European mythology and was mentioned by Pliny the Elder as far back as the 1st century AD. It is so venomous that a look alone is enough to kill a man, and its fiery breath can kill birds. The only creature that can kill it is the weasel. The ball and socket joints used for its body mean it can pose like a real serpent.

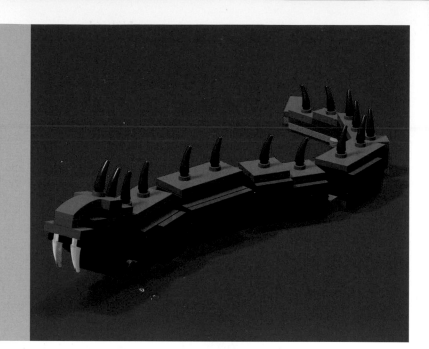

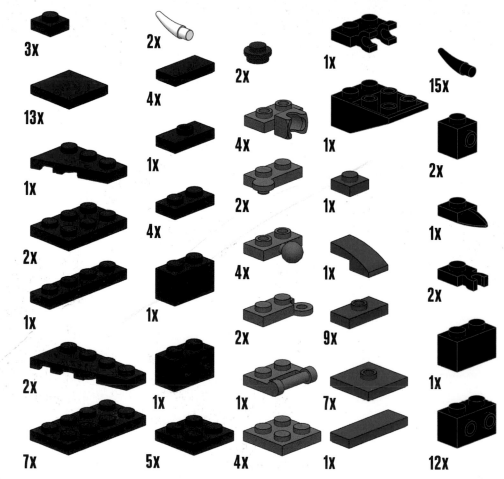

3x

2x

2x

1x

15x

13x

4x

4x

1x

2x

1x

4x

1x

4x

2x

1x

1x

2x

4x

1x

1x

1x

2x

2x

2x

9x

1x

2x

1x

1x

7x

1x

7x

5x

4x

1x

12x

BASILISK

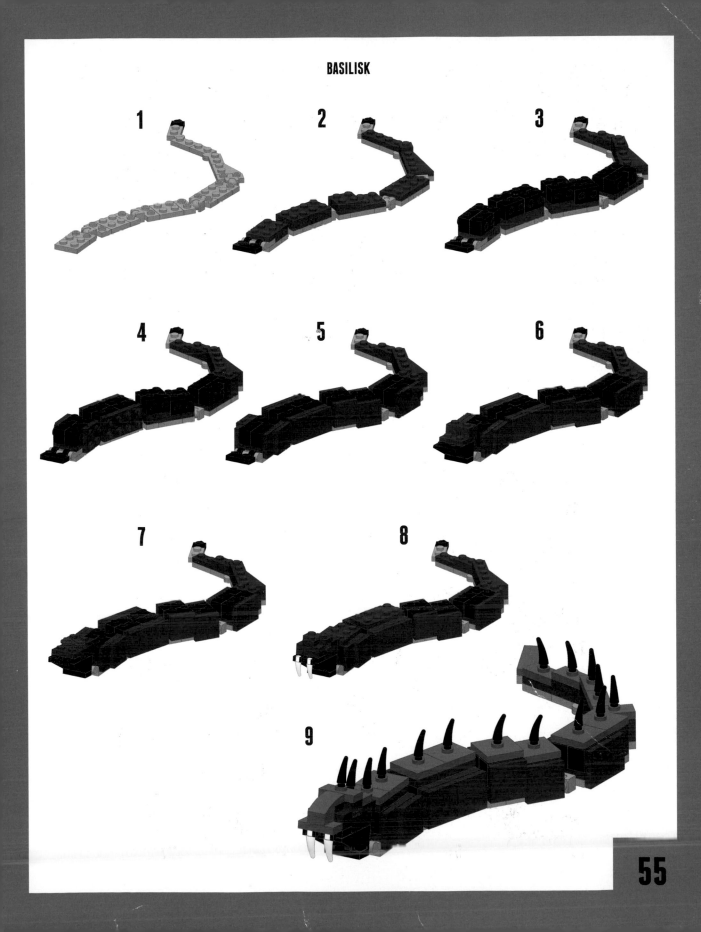

elf

These mysterious beings are said to have supernatural beauty and magical powers. They are all different, and while some might help people (think of Christmas elves), others might lead people into harm's way. I've used two tail tips connected with a 1 × 1 plate with a lamp holder to make his bow.

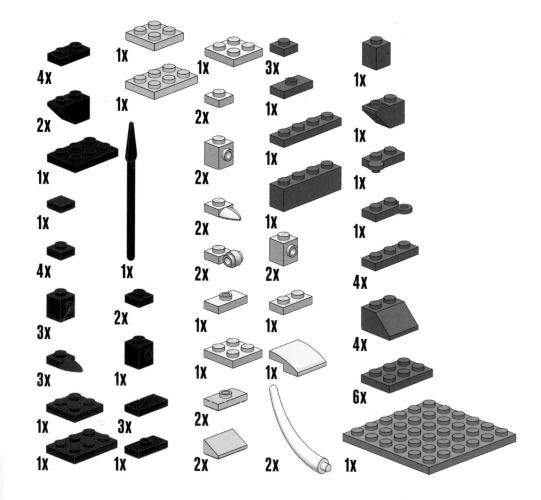

4x

1x

1x

1x

3x

1x

2x

2x

1x

1x

1x

2x

1x

2x

2x

2x

1x

4x

3x

1x

1x

2x

1x

3x

1x

1x

1x

1x

1x

4x

4x

6x

1x

2x

2x

1x

drop bear

The fearsome drop bear is a large and vicious koala-like animal that lives in the treetops of Australia. It attacks its prey (often people) by dropping onto it as it passes below. A creature of modern mythology, its story is often told to tourists. My model's realistically koala-like nose is made using a 1 × 2 curved brick.

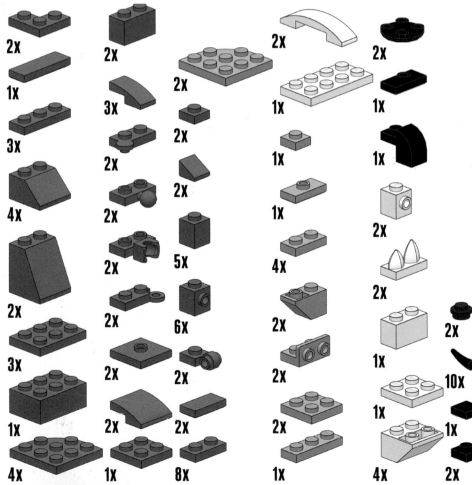

DROP BEAR

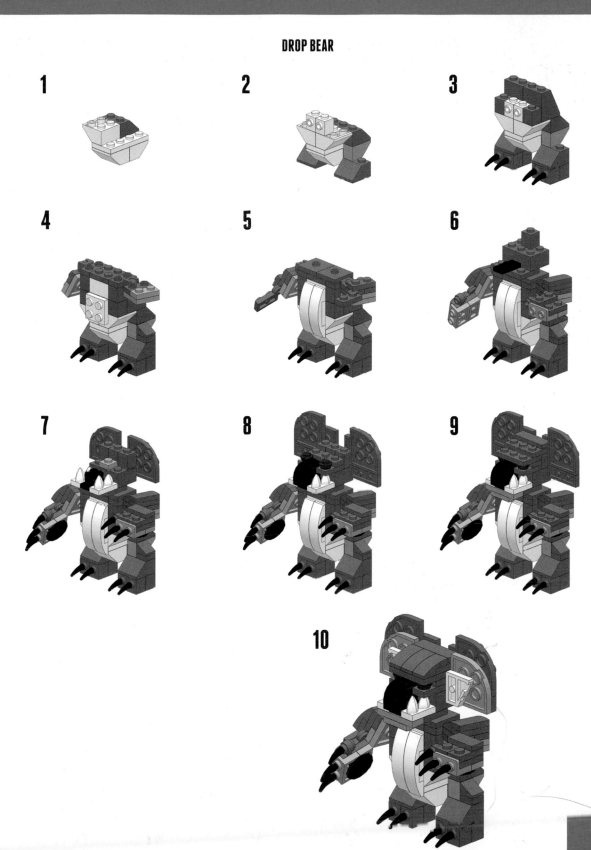

cerberus

This monstrous three-headed dog guards the gates of the Underworld (Hades) in Greek mythology. He allows the dead to enter, but makes sure they never leave. In some depictions, he is given more than three heads and sometimes also has a serpent's tail and a lion's mane. The points of his teeth fit neatly into the underside of a plate so he can have an impressively beastly bite.

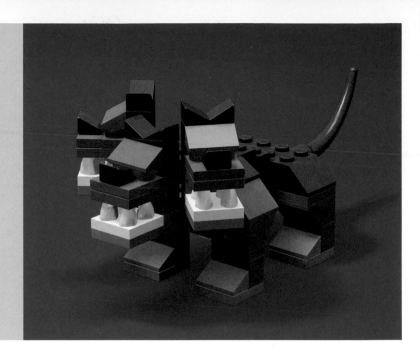

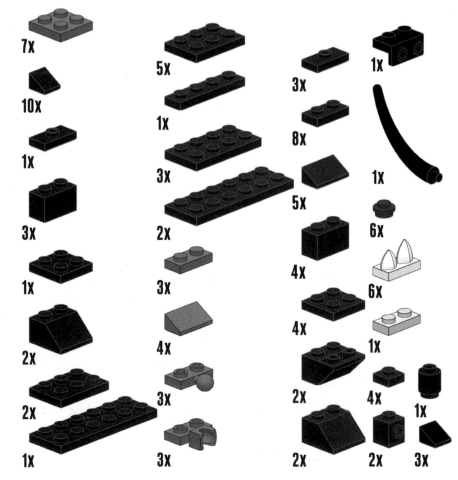

7x

10x

1x

3x

1x

2x

2x

1x

5x

1x

3x

2x

3x

4x

3x

3x

3x

8x

5x

4x

2x

2x

1x

1x

6x

6x

1x

4x

2x

1x

2x

3x

CERBERUS

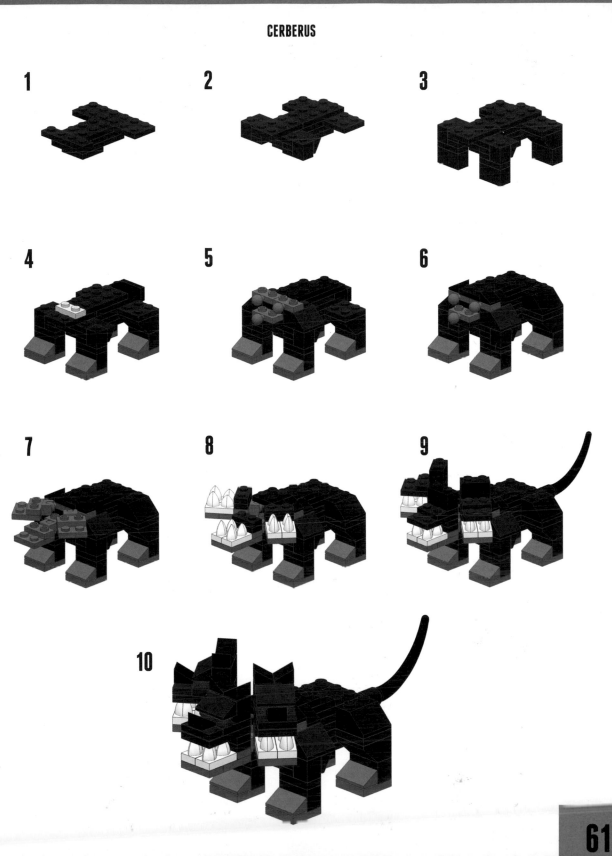

griffin

This legendary creature is a royal animal mash up. It has the body, tail, and back legs of a lion (the king of the beasts) and the head and wings of an eagle (the king of the skies), with an eagle's talons on its front paws. It is a majestic creature that is often used to guard precious goods. I've used tooth plates to give the appearance of feathers on its wings.

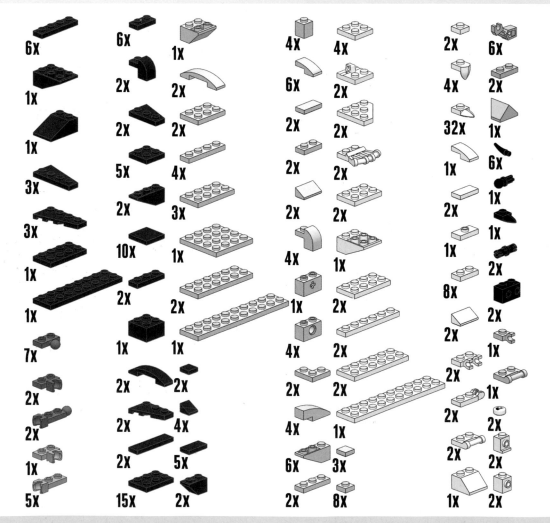

6x 6x 1x 4x 4x 2x 6x

1x 2x 2x 6x 2x 4x 2x

1x 2x 2x 2x 2x 32x 1x

3x 5x 4x 2x 2x 1x 6x

3x 2x 3x 2x 2x 2x 1x

1x 10x 1x 4x 1x 1x 1x

1x 2x 2x 1x 2x 1x 2x

7x 1x 1x 4x 2x 8x 2x

2x 2x 2x 2x 2x 2x 1x

2x 2x 4x 2x 2x 2x 1x

1x 2x 5x 4x 1x 2x 2x

5x 15x 2x 6x 3x 2x 2x

2x 8x 1x 2x

GRIFFIN

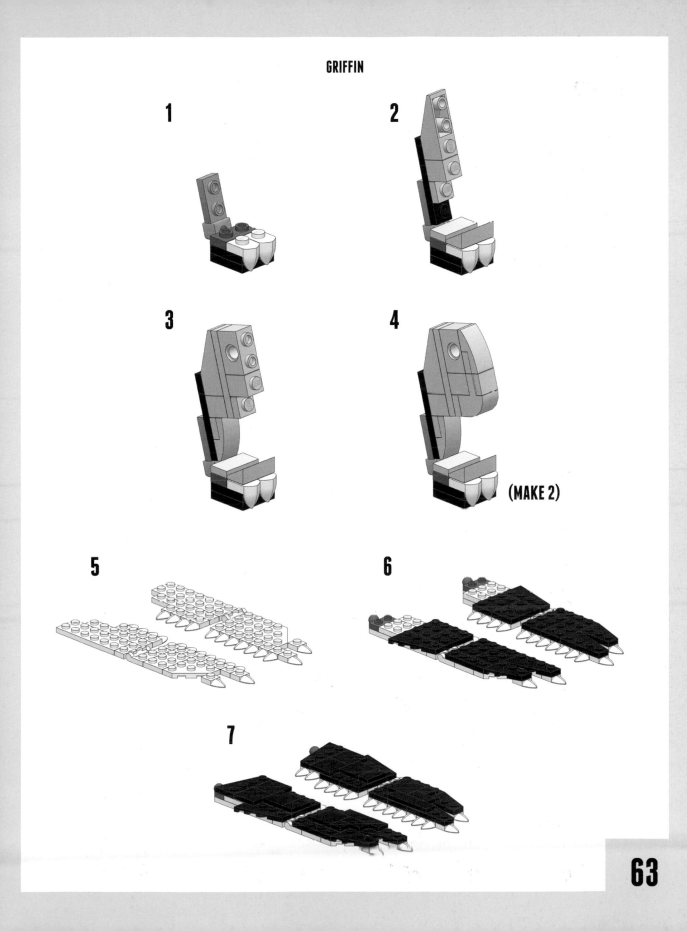

1

2

3

4

(MAKE 2)

5

6

7

sasquatch

Also known as Bigfoot, Sasquatch is a large, hairy, ape-like creature that lives in the forests of North America. He walks on two legs, and his footprints are said to be as much as two feet long, which explains his alternative name. I've used 1 × 2 inverse slopes to make the model's feet big enough!

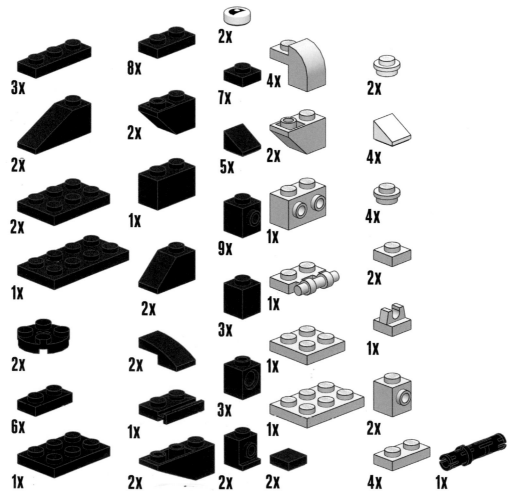

SASQUATCH

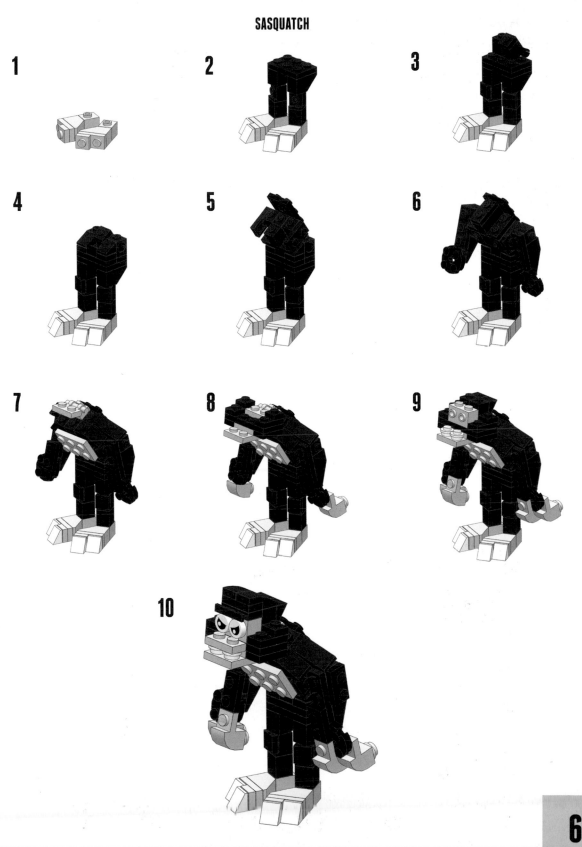

1

2

3

4

5

6

7

8

9

10

ogre

Huge, galumphing, and with a fondness for eating children, an ogre is something you wouldn't want to bump into on a dark night—or any night, for that matter. They often have an unusual skin color, so be creative when picking out your LEGO® bricks. I've used headlight bricks on his jaw so that his teeth can point upward from his mouth in true ogre style.

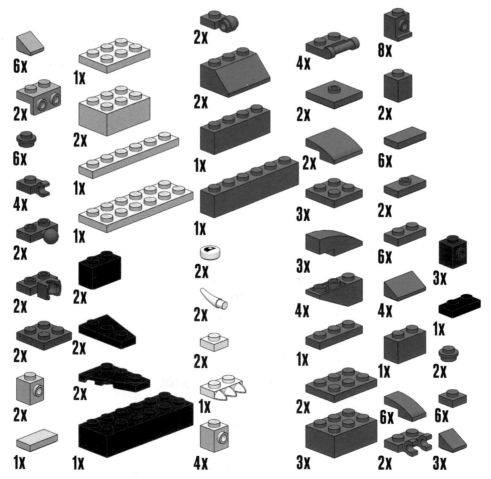

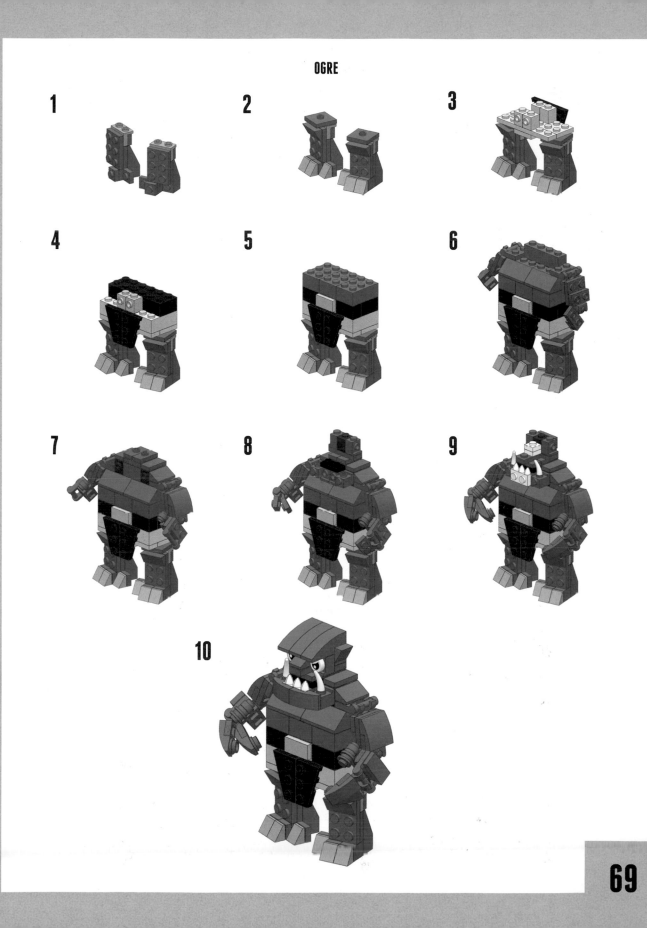

Al-mi'raj

This beast from Arabian mythology has a two-foot spiraling horn on its head and is found on a mysterious island in the Indian Ocean. It might look like a little bunny, but there is nothing sweet about its ferocious appetite and its ability to kill animals several times its own size. Curved slopes spaced out on a 1 × 3 plate mean each ear can be angled independently.

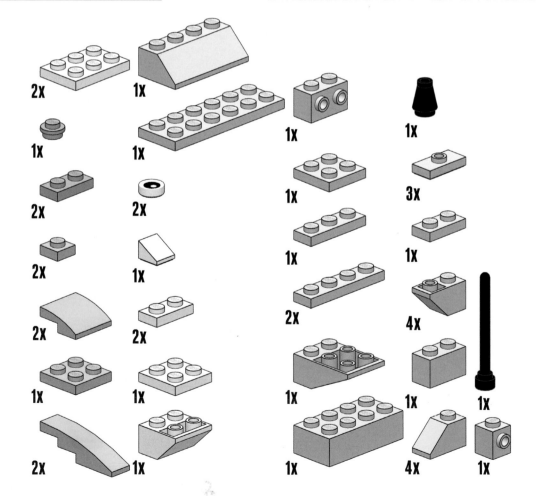

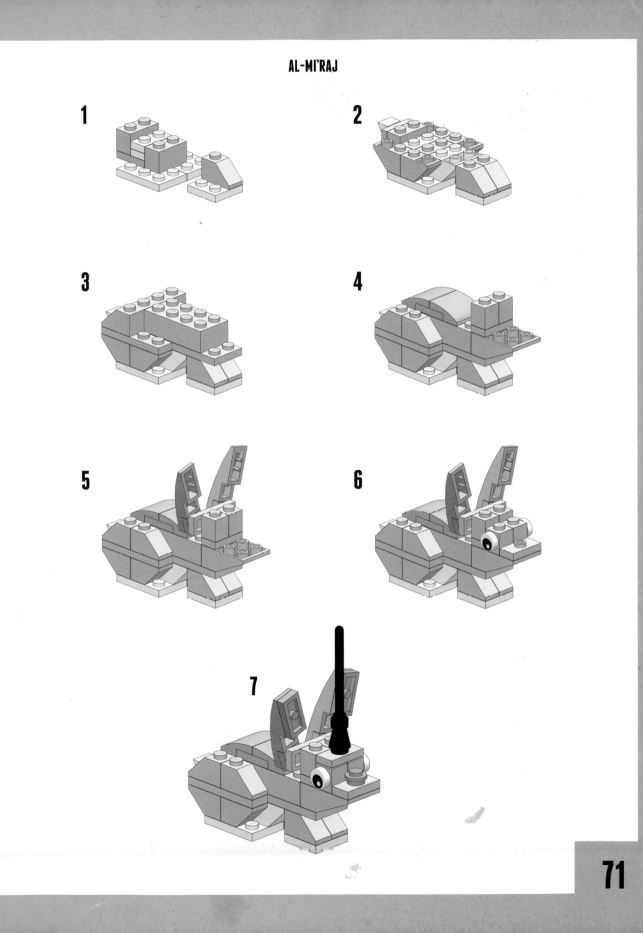

1

2

3

4

5

6

7

shi (guardian lion)

These elaborate lions stand in front of the gates of many imperial palaces and important buildings in China and across Asia. Usually seen in pairs, the male lion often has his front paw on an embroidered ball, representing his dominance over the world, while the female has her paw on a cub, representing the cycle of life.

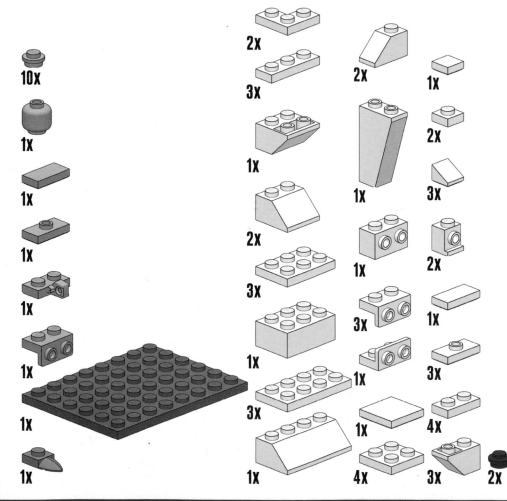

SHI (GUARDIAN LION)

1

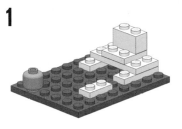

2

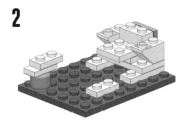

3

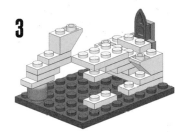

4

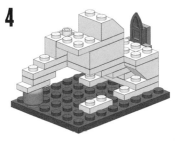

5

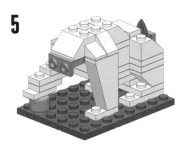

6

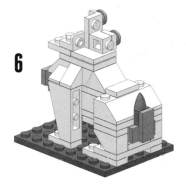

7

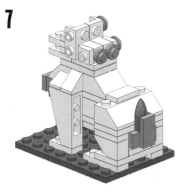

8

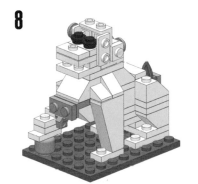

9

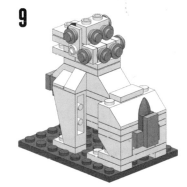

10

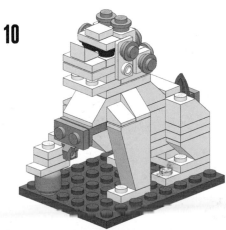

dwarf

This small person is often associated with wisdom as well as with the professions of smithing and mining. Dwarves first appeared in German mythology but have since cropped up in plenty of modern literature. A 1 x 2 curved brick turned sideways makes the model look as if his hand is wrapped around the axe handle.

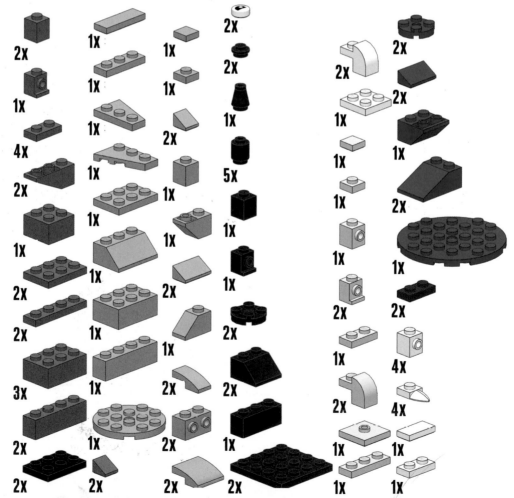

DWARF

hodag

With the head of a frog, thick short legs with huge claws as toes, spikes along its back, and a tail with spears at the end, the hodag is an ugly and fearsome creature. It lives in the woods around the town of Rhinelander in Wisconsin, and is said to eat only white bulldogs. The head is given its rounded shape using curved slopes at different levels.

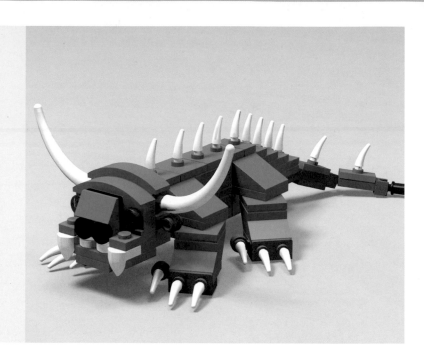

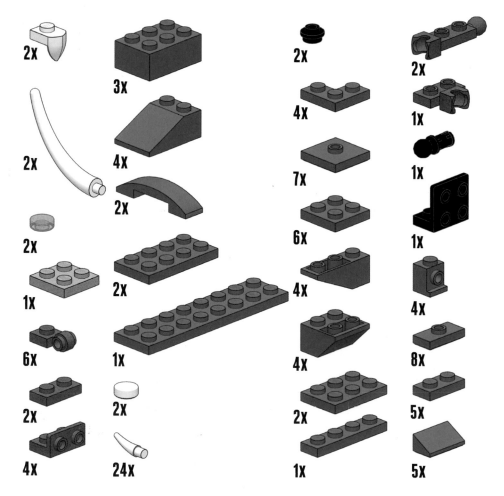

2x

3x

2x

4x

2x

2x

1x

2x

6x

1x

2x

2x

4x

24x

2x

4x

7x

6x

4x

4x

2x

1x

2x

2x

1x

1x

4x

8x

5x

5x

HODAG

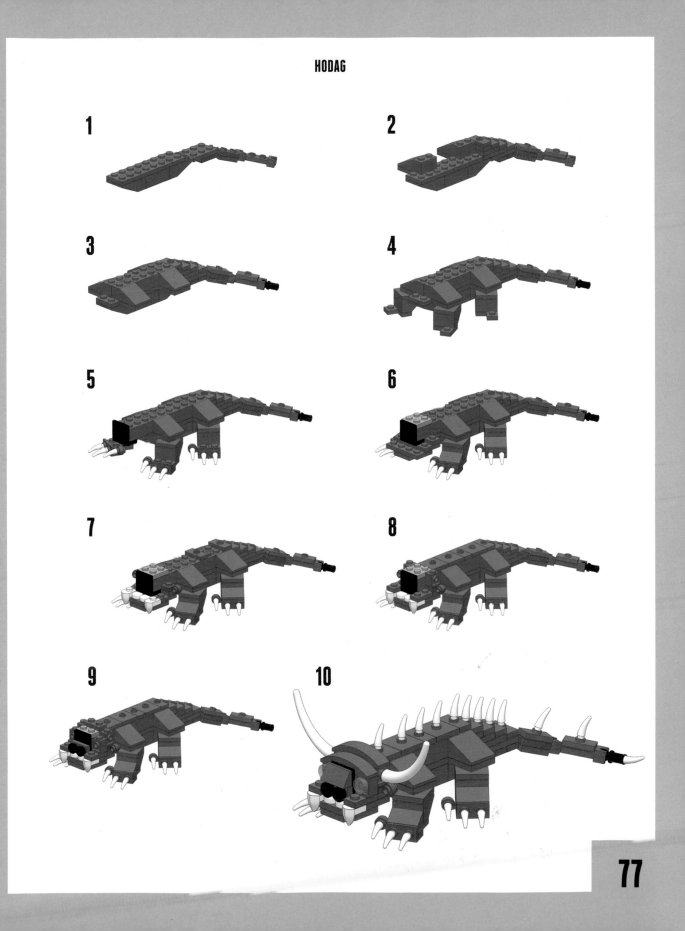

yeti

From the folklore of Nepal, the yeti is a large, hairy, ape-like creature that walks on two legs. Ancient people of the Himalayas worshipped the animal as a "glacier being." In English, its name is sometimes given as the Abominable Snowman. Give the body its bulky appearance using basic bricks.

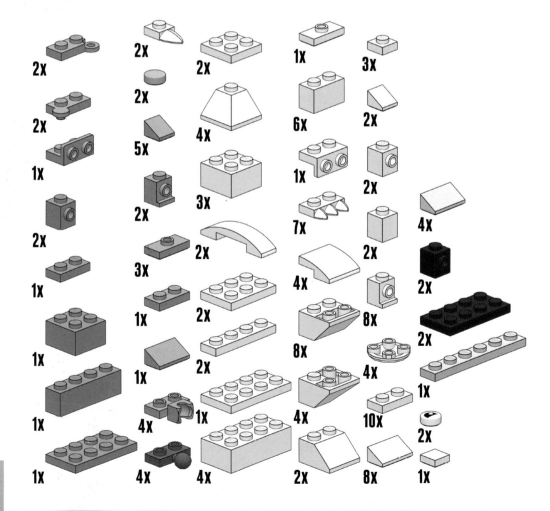

2x 2x 2x 1x 3x

2x 2x 4x 6x 2x

1x 5x 3x 1x 2x

2x 2x 2x 7x 4x

1x 3x 4x 2x

1x 1x 2x 4x 8x 2x

1x 2x 8x 4x 1x

1x 4x 1x 4x 10x 2x

1x 4x 4x 2x 8x 1x

YETI

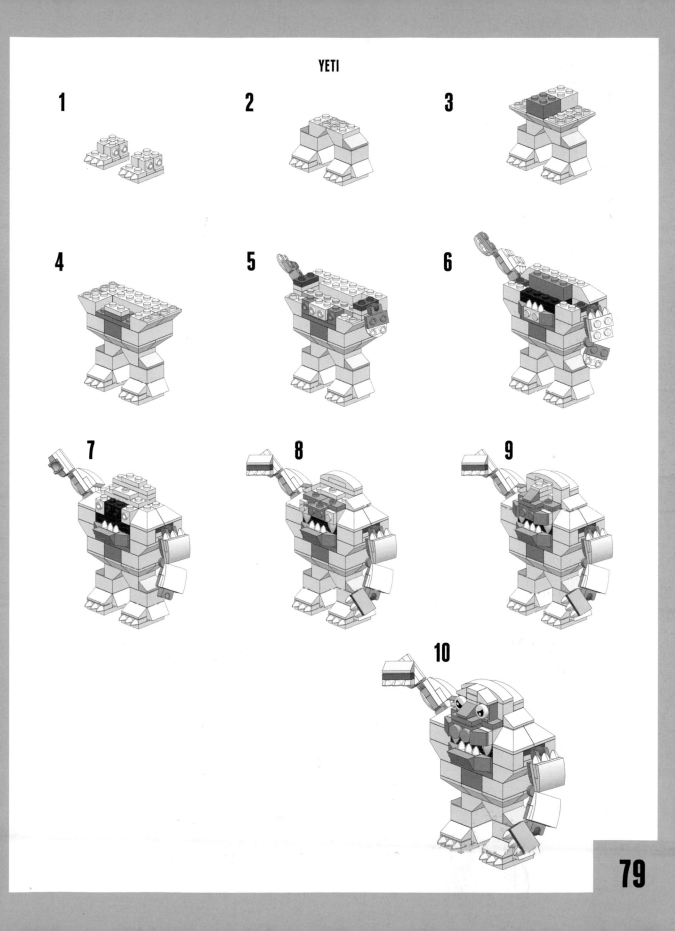

treefolk

While some treefolk can look almost entirely like a human, others are more like trees, with facial features made from knots and branches and with the ability to uproot themselves and walk. They are often found near fairy rings. Using different shades of brown makes the trunk look more realistic. Its mouth is made from a plate on a vertical clip so it can move.

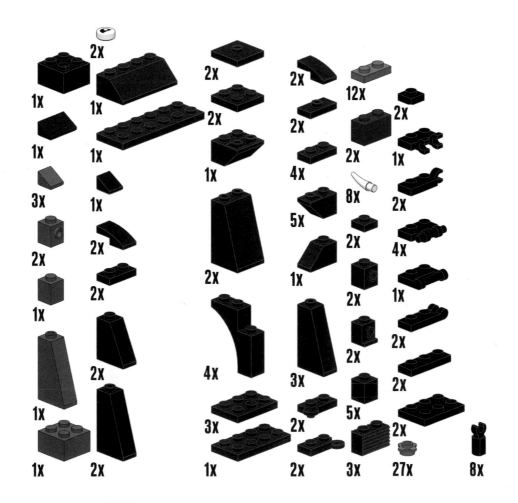

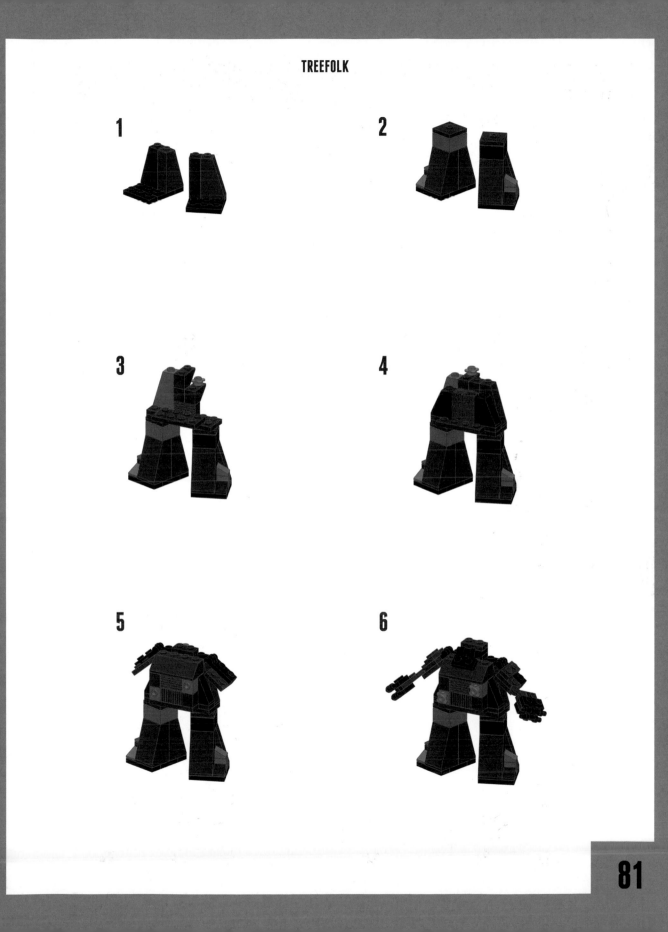

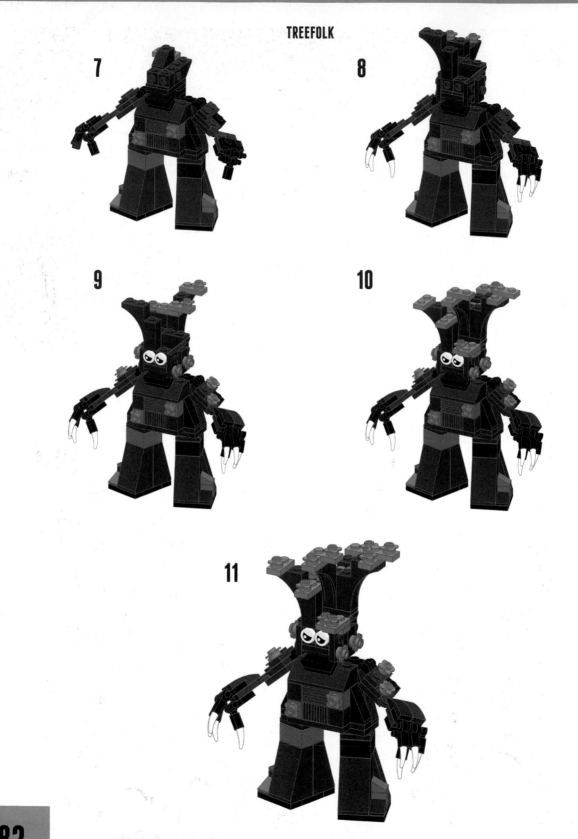

hydra

The Hydra is a deadly, many-headed water monster of Greek mythology. For every head her attackers cut off, another two grow. The Greek god Hercules eventually slew the Hydra, which can now be seen as a constellation in the night sky. Create her fearsome eyes using two 1 × 1 plates stacked together.

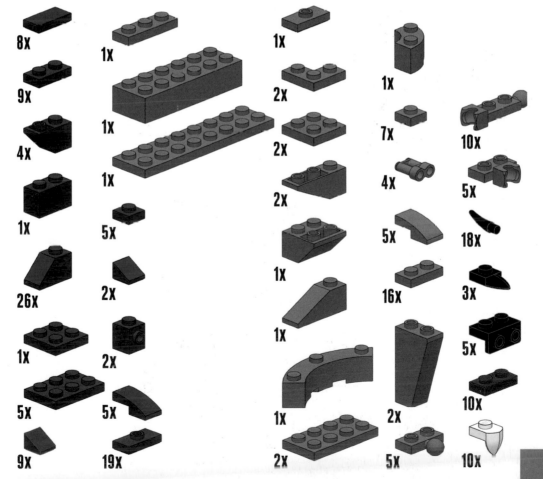

8x
9x
4x
1x
26x
1x
5x
9x

1x
1x
1x
5x
2x
2x
5x
19x

1x
2x
2x
2x
1x
1x
1x
2x

1x
7x
4x
5x
16x
2x
5x

1x
10x
5x
18x
3x
5x
10x
10x

HYDRA

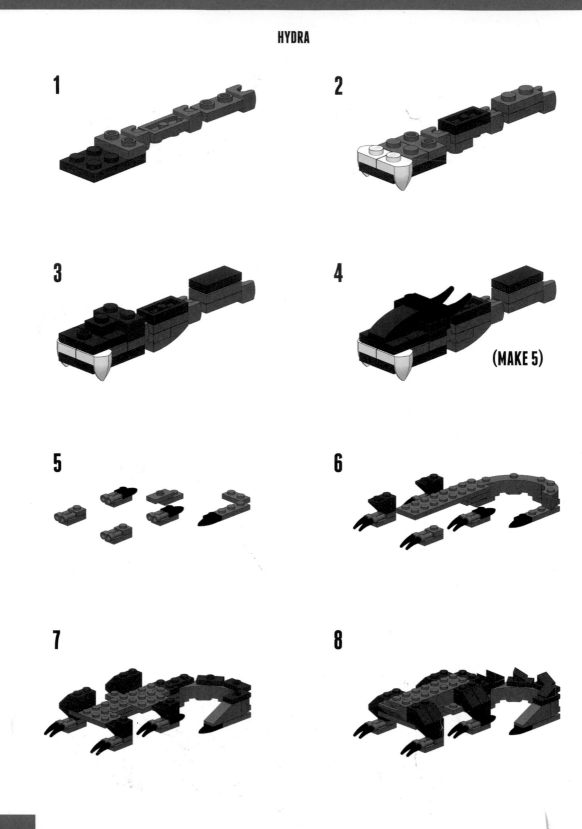

1

2

3

4 (MAKE 5)

5

6

7

8

9

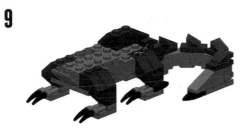

10

11

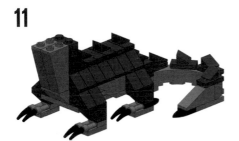

12

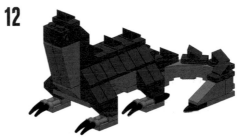

13

14

werewolf

Werewolves are humans who can transform into wolves, complete with all the vicious characteristics that wolves have. It is often said that werewolf transformation only takes place on the night of a full moon. The 1 × 1 slopes on the side of its head make it look as if its fur is sticking up.

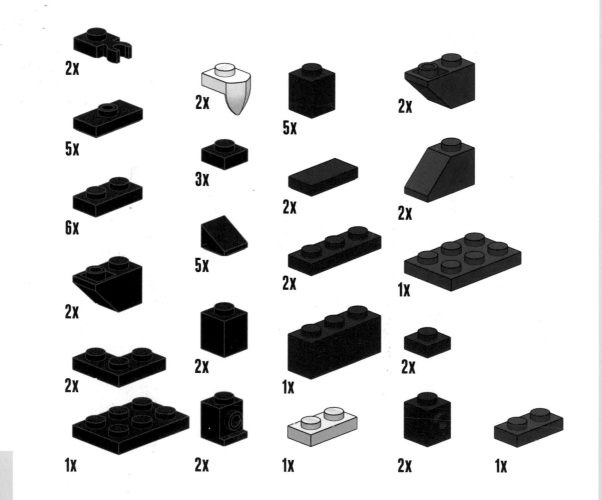

2x

2x

5x

2x

5x

3x

2x

2x

6x

5x

2x

2x

2x

2x

1x

2x

1x

2x

1x

2x

1x

2x

1x

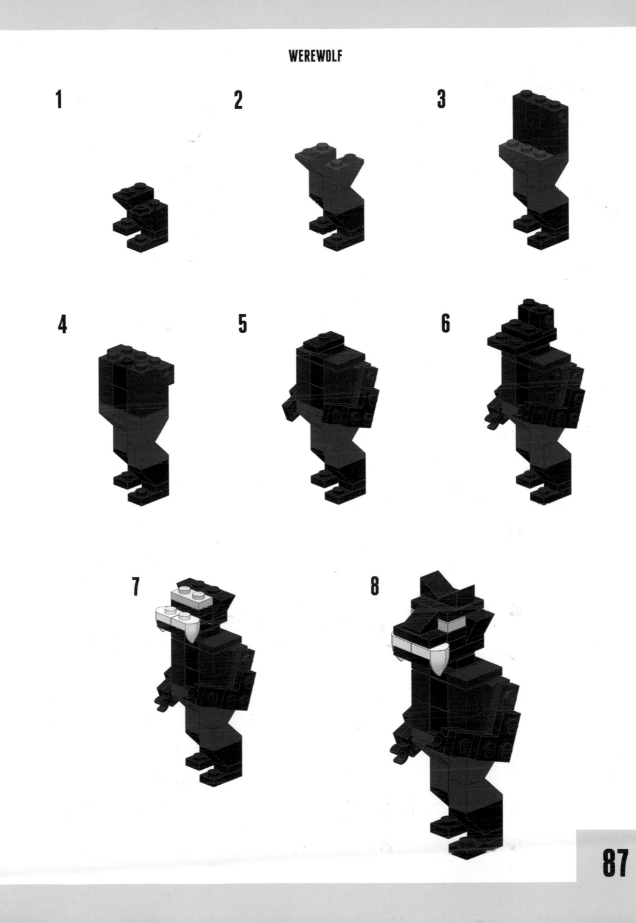

centaur

A stalwart of Greek mythology, the centaur has the upper body of a man and the lower body of a horse. They are generally portrayed as being wild like untamed horses and ferocious in battle. The Sagittarius zodiac sign is often represented by the famous centaur Chiron, who mentored Greek hero Achilles in archery. I've made the long hair by using 1 × 1 bricks with a stud on the side and then by attaching plates horizontally.

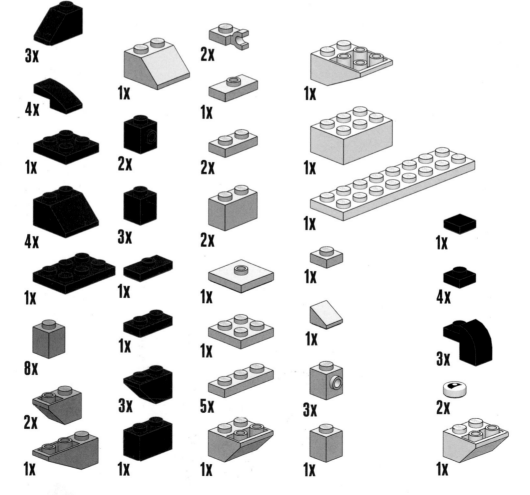

CENTAUR

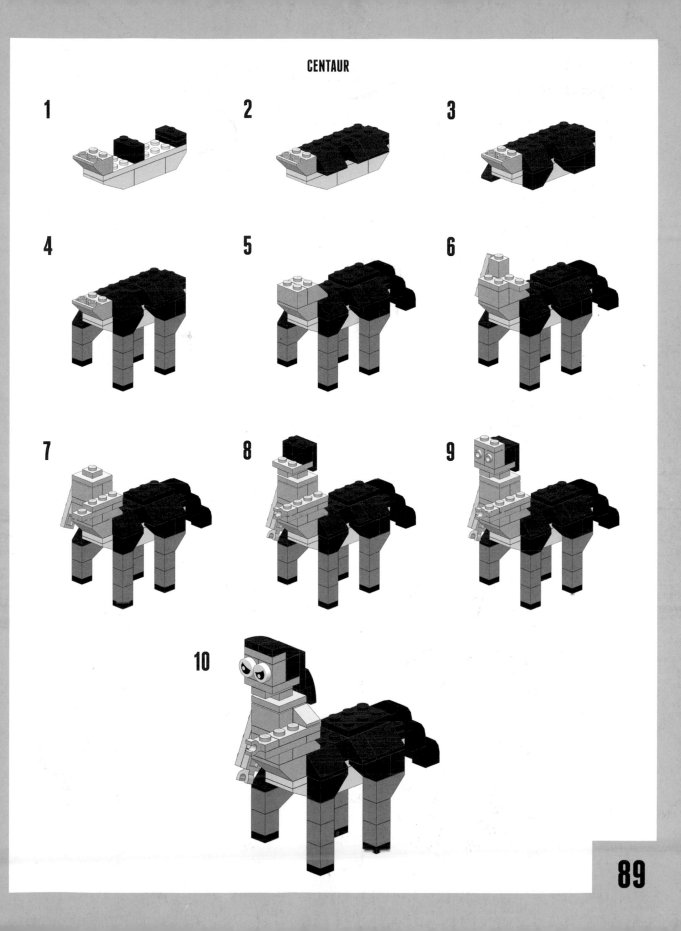

manticore

The name *manticore* derives from the Persian for *man-eater*. It is a beast to be feared, with the body of a lion and a scorpion-like tail that can fire spikes at its enemies. In its mouth it has three rows of teeth like a shark. You can make a realistic scorpion's tail by using the ball and socket 1 × 2 plates to bring the tail up and over the body.

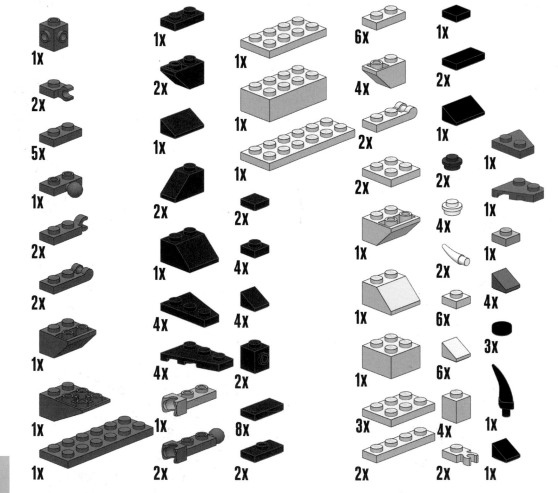

MANTICORE

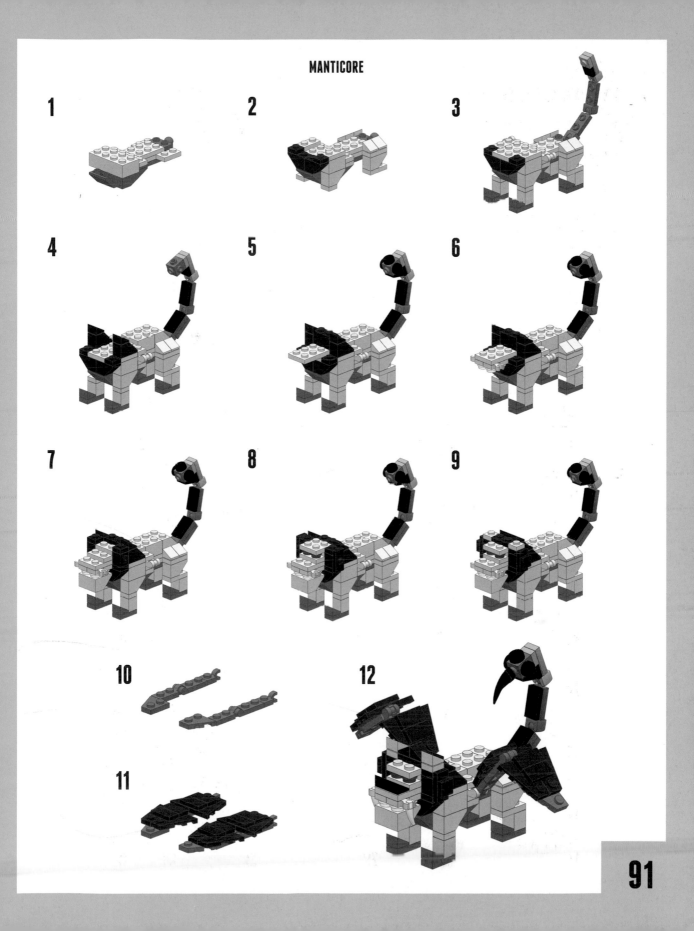

1

2

3

4

5

6

7

8

9

10

11

12

pegasus

Pegasus is the winged white stallion that features throughout Greek myths. He was captured and tamed by the Greek hero Bellerophon, who rode Pegasus into battle against the fire-breathing monster Chimera. Using a 6 × 6 base plate lets you pose the model as if it's rearing up into the air.

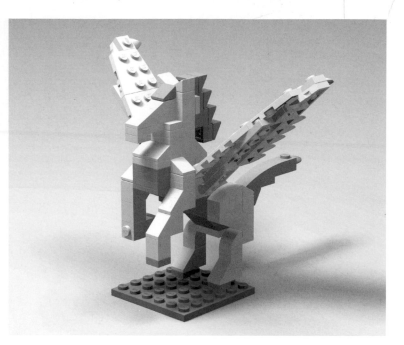

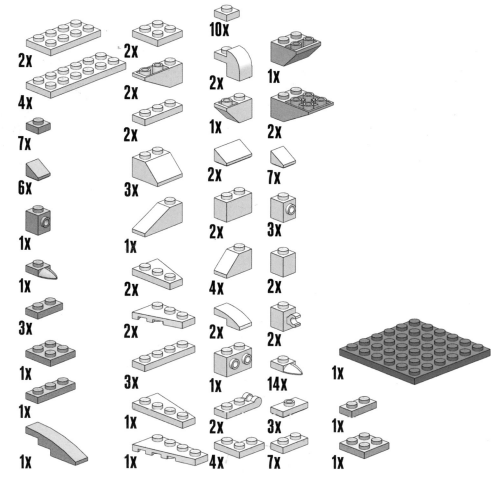

2X
4X
7X
6X
1X
1X
3X
1X
1X
1X

2X
2X
2X
3X
1X
2X
2X
3X
1X
1X

10X
2X
1X
2X
4X
2X
2X
1X
2X
3X
4X

1X
2X
7X
2X
3X
2X
2X
14X
3X
7X

1X
1X
1X

PEGASUS

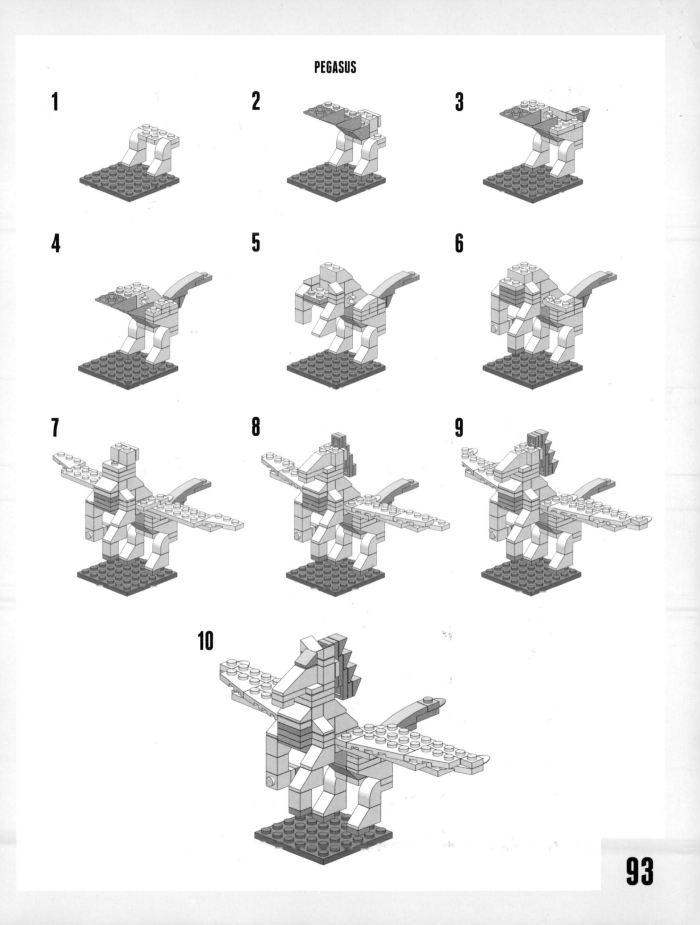

loch ness monster

Affectionately known as Nessie, the Loch Ness Monster has reportedly been sighted in Scotland's Loch Ness for hundreds of years. She is always referred to as female and has a long neck and a number of humps that protrude out of the water. These can be made using 1 x 4 arched bricks.

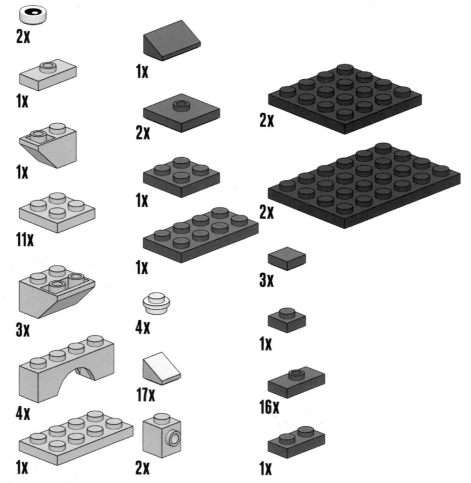

2x

1x

1x

1x

11x

3x

4x

1x

1x

2x

1x

1x

4x

17x

2x

2x

2x

1x

2x

3x

1x

16x

1x

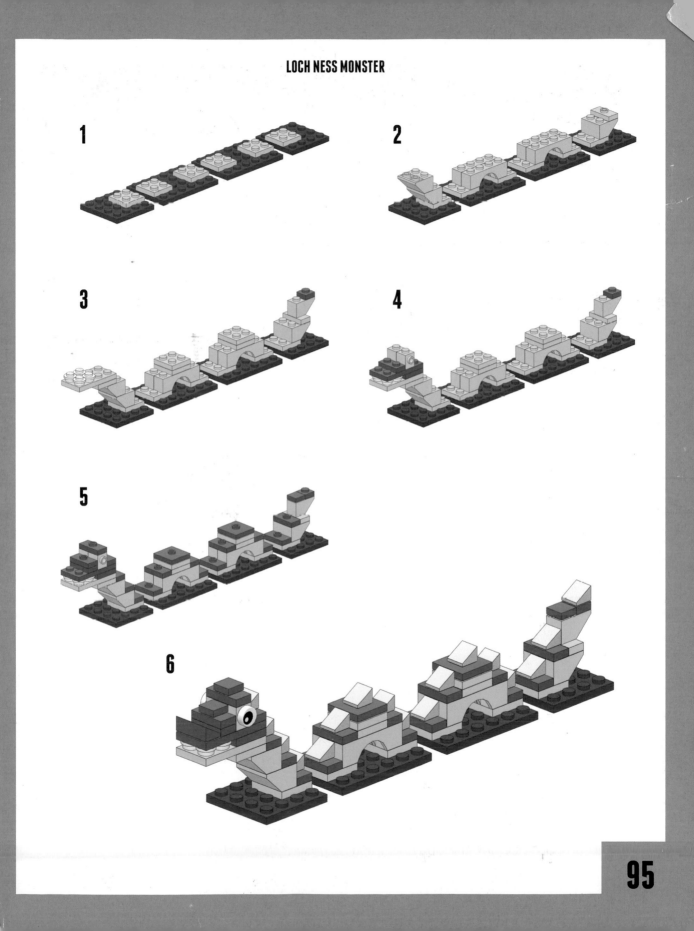

credits

Kevin Hall is a cofounder of Brick Galleria—a LEGO® brick model building design and events company—and a professional LEGO brick artist. He designs, develops, and creates LEGO brick models for companies, events, promotions, and collectors. He has been part of the international LEGO community since 2000, creating models and sculptures and designing custom collector figurines, bespoke sets, graphics, and promotional material for events around the world. His models have been featured in television advertising campaigns, toy fairs, exhibitions, print media, and theme parks, and have been used by government organizations. He recently turned his hand to writing and his work was featured in the official LEGO book, *365 Things to Do with LEGO Bricks,* which won the "Best Book" category in the Creative Play Awards 2016 in the United Kingdom. He also organizes and runs LEGO workshops for children and corporate groups. Before becoming a professional LEGO brick artist, Kevin spent three decades in the advertising industry in various creative incarnations.

Brenda Tsang is a cofounder of Brick Galleria. This followed fifteen years of creating and managing products for global entertainment brands. Brenda is passionate about creating products that have cutting-edge functionality, are aesthetically pleasing, and stand out from the crowd. She also specializes in scenery art and spatial design, which enables her to create the enhanced experience of Brick Galleria events. Brenda helped on the research and design for models in this book and with selecting LEGO parts for some of the finer details.

Barry James assists Brick Galleria with its workshops and creating LEGO models. When not doing this, he builds from his imagination and shares images of his models on Instagram. He has a particular talent for mixing models with real-world locations and so never travels without a box of assorted mini-figures and a camera in case a photo opportunity pops into his head. He helped design models for this book and built the models for the photographs.